MEDIA MINISTRY
Made Easy

A Practical Guide to Visual Communication

"This easy read is full of practical answers to the usual set of questions real practitioners ask about media ministry. A valuable contribution to the mission of media in the church from one of the most pioneering, knowledgeable, and affable servants we know." **—Len Wilson and Jason Moore**

Jason Moore and **Len Wilson** have been media ministry pioneers since 1993 in such places as Ginghamsburg Church near Dayton, Ohio and Lumicon Digital Productions in Dallas. Their current ministry, www.MidnightOilProductions.net, aims to provide teaching, speaking, and resources for churches using media in ministry.

"Many of us fear the unknown...if we don't understand it, we're not sure we can implement it. Tim's work gently allays the fears around media ministry and creates an environment of understanding. You'll come away from this book thinking, "Hey, we can do this!" **—Kim Miller**

Kim Miller is Creative Director at Ginghamsburg Church in Tipp City, Ohio where she and the worship team work to create an atmosphere where people can experience God.

"In a world of visual learners, sound bytes, and shortened attention spans, media is a non-negotiable. However, many church leaders don't know where to begin. They feel inadequate and overwhelmed by the high-tech world of media. Like an experienced "Sherpa," Tim Eason guides us through the dangers and complexities of implementing a media ministry...." **—Lance Witt**

Lance Witt serves as Teaching Pastor, and Pastor of Discipleship and Small Groups at Saddleback Church in Southern California.

"Tim Eason doesn't cut corners in his honesty about media ministry on the costs in time, equipment, and people or on the necessity of a guiding biblical vision. Starting a media ministry? Read this book!" **—Yvon Prehn**

Yvon Prehn is a speaker, writer, and consultant who specializes in ministry-driven Christian communication seminars and marketing. (www.cyberservant.org)

"If we're going to reach a sight and sound generation with a message of hope, we'll have to use the media to do it. Media Ministry Made Easy *is a great place to start. Every church in America should be reading this."* **—Phil Cooke**

Phil Cooke is a producer and director who has been breaking the rules for more than two decades in order to reach an audience with impact. (www.cookefilm.com)

"Media Ministry Made Easy provides relevant and realistic steps for churches who are ready to take the digital dive." **—Anthony D. Coppedge, CTS**

Anthony Coppedge is a renowned speaker and sought-after consultant in the church A/V marketplace.

"In a world of increasingly image-rich communication, church leaders must become familiar with the skills and tools of the current culture of multimedia. This resource guide is filled with the information, tools, and directions needed to develop a serious media ministry. Tim Eason knows his stuff!" **—Rob Weber**

Rob Weber is senior pastor and founder of Grace Community United Methodist Church in Shreveport, Louisiana.

"This book promises to be an indispensable handbook for multisensory worship. Both the novice and the expert will benefit from its informative and practical counsel." **—Linda McCoy**

Linda McCoy is Pastor of The Garden and The Garden at Oak Hill, Blossoms of St. Luke's United Methodist Church, Indianapolis, Indiana.

Media Ministry
Made Easy

A Practical Guide to Visual Communication

Tim Eason

Abingdon Press

Nashville, Tennessee

MEDIA MINISTRY MADE EASY:
A PRACTICAL GUIDE TO VISUAL COMMUNICATION

Copyright © 2003 Tim Eason

This book is printed on acid-free, recycled paper.

ISBN 0-687-02578-8

Adobe, the Adobe logo, Adobe Premiere, Adobe Photoshop, and Adobe Elements are trademarks of Adobe Systems Incorporated.

Microsoft, Microsoft Office, PowerPoint, and PowerPoint Viewer are registered trademarks of Microsoft Corporation.

DIRECTOR® © 1984-2000, Macromedia, Inc.

Macintosh® and QuickTime® are registered trademarks of Apple Computer, Inc.

Other product and company names mentioned herein may be the trademarks of their respective owners.

03 04 05 06 07 08 09 10 11 12—10 9 8 7 6 5 4 3 2 1

MANUFACTURED IN THE UNITED STATES OF AMERICA

This book is dedicated to hard-working media ministers everywhere, to those on staff, to all indispensable volunteers, and to all servants who have a genuine calling to serve the Kingdom of God through the giving of their technical and creative talents.

Contents

Acknowledgments

Special thanks to the companies that contributed to the resources on the DVD:

Adobe Systems Incorporated
345 Park Avenue
San Jose, CA 95110-2704
800-833-6687
www.adobe.com

Artbeats Software Inc.
Box 709
Myrtle Creek, OR 97457
800-444-9392
www.artbeats.com

David Delgado
www.daviddelgado.com

DONline Solutions
13839 Chisom St. Suite 102
San Antonio, TX 78249
877-690-4462
www.worshipbuilder.com

Grass Roots Software
2015 Airpark Court
Auburn, CA 95602
877-274-7277
www.sundayplus.com

Highway Video
201 Castro St., 3rd floor
Mountain View, CA 94041
800-693-4449
www.highwayvideo.com

Jim Whitmer Photography
125 Wakeman Ave.
Wheaton, IL 60187
888-653-1344
www.worshipphotos.com

Matrox Electronic Systems Ltd
1055 St. Regis Blvd.
Dorval, Québec
Canada H9P 2T4
514-822-6000
www.matrox.com

MediaComplete Corporation
P.O. Box 24625
Nashville, TN 37202
888-829-7168
www.mediashout.com

Parting Water
P.O. Box 53912
Lubbock, TX 79453
800-999-5266
www.partingwater.com

Royalty Free Stuff
888-937-9473
www.royaltyfreestuff.com

Softouch Development
Softouch Development, Inc.
8023 E. 63rd Pl. Suite 255
Tulsa, OK 74133-1243
888-876-4004
www.easyworship.com

VideoAnimation
2269 South University Drive #132
Davie, FL 33324
877-259-9718
www.videoanimation.com

Video Scriptures
www.video4worship.com

Visual Worship
PO Box 2436
Evansville IN 47728-0436
812-402-1237
www.visualworship.com

WorshipBacks
www.worshipbacks.com

Introduction

Imagine, for a moment, that Jesus' first coming did not happen 2,000 years ago. From an historical point of view we know that Jesus' timing was perfect, but if you are convinced that Christ is relevant in the present day envision a twenty-first century version of Jesus.

Extrapolate from the Scriptures what we know about Jesus. He was a cutting-edge communicator. He knew how to reach an audience and hold their attention by using parables, word pictures, and stories. He spoke of everyday life and related to the culture at their level.

So many times we read of Jesus' storytelling without picturing what He may have been doing as He told the tales. Jesus was obviously very creative and imaginative. Perhaps Jesus used props to help the listener visualize messages about faith and justice. I'm confidant that Jesus was dramatic as He captivated the audience with suspenseful and sometimes entertaining narratives. It's no wonder people gathered around Jesus to hear Him speak!

So, if Jesus walked this planet for the first time today, what would the Christ be like? I'm convinced of several attributes that Jesus would have. He would be a fun person. He would be entertaining, while at the same time he would bring insightful and meaningful messages that relate to people. Jesus would definitely have a first-rate website. He would take advantage of every visual technology available. He would be toting a laptop computer and video projector to relate the messages. He might even be a movie producer!

Take a close look at our culture and the dominant forms of communication in our world. Television, movies, the Internet, and music each play vital roles in our society. These powerful methods of telling stories have influenced human lives more effectively than any other means of communication ever known to humankind. The Church has the awesome responsibility of taking the message of Christ to all nations. If we are going to accomplish this great commission, we must take advantage of the tools available to us that will allow us to communicate more effectively and in a way that is relevant to our society.

In recent years, churches all over the globe have implemented video projection into their worship services. Just as Gutenberg's printing press revolutionized the distribution of the Bible, video projectors are revolutionizing communication in the Church. The cost of the equipment needed for creating and displaying media continues to drop, making media ministry affordable for almost any size church. Although the technology has become more accessible, many churches using media are not taking full advantage of the potential of this powerful form of communication. This book is intended to equip and motivate you to effectively use media as a tool for ministry, just as I believe Jesus would do if ministering in the flesh on earth today.

Section 1: Implementing an Effective Media Ministry

Chapter 1
Motivations for Using Media

Media is a broad term and can mean anything from print to broadcasting to journalism. For the purposes of this book, we have defined media as computer-generated slides, graphics, and videos to be shown on a large screen via a video projector. The methods described may also be applied to broadcasting on television. The focus, however, will be on incorporating these techniques for in-house applications within the church.

There are several key motivations for using media in the church. First, visually reinforcing the spoken word can *increase retention*. Without thinking too hard about it, do you remember what last week's sermon was about? I ask this question at my seminars and seldom get more than two or three people who can remember the sermon topic from a few days earlier. What is even more disappointing is that those two or three people are the pastors that preached the sermons! The sad fact is that most people cannot remember a sermon the day after it is preached. What a loss! Pastors may spend hours praying and preparing for a message, only for it to be a vague memory the day after it is delivered. Numerous studies have shown that using visual media to reinforce a message can increase retention by over fifty percent. At the same time, it provides a more dynamic environment for learning and worship.

Media is the *ultimate tool for communication* in today's culture. I believe that never before in the history of the Church have we had access to such powerful means of communicating. The projector may be used as a conduit for art and the screen may be thought of as a blank painting canvas—a canvas that may be used over and over again and change at a moment's notice. The projection screen has also been compared to a modern-day stained glass window. In earlier era, stained glass windows were used to tell stories, particularly Bible stories, to the vast majority of the population who could not read or afford to buy a copy of the Bible. Our modern-day version of the stained glass window can tell a multitude of stories, all with action and even sound. Once mastered, using media can deliver a message with tremendous impact.

It is a popular belief among those involved in media ministry that media *is the language of our culture.* My parents, Thomas and Betty Eason, are originally from Alabama in the "Deep South." Like any area of the country, the South has its unique culture. Generations of Easons were born and raised in the South, and this way of life was all that my parents knew. In 1967 they felt a call into mission work and specifically to work with Spanish-speaking people at a time when there were virtually no Hispanic populations in the South. Imagine two Southerners wanting to reach a culture that they knew nothing about, including the language. To learn to communicate, my parents spent a year in language school to learn Spanish. They moved to a part of the country that was completely foreign to them (New Mexico). They left behind everything that they had grown up with to reach this specific culture. It was definitely not an easy thing to do, but in order to reach the people you must speak the language.

The language of media is foreign to many pastors who may have not been exposed to this method of communication in their training. If the church wants to reach new generations of believers, it must learn to speak this new language fluently. Just as it was a big step for my parents to leave the South behind, church leaders must also step outside their comfort zone to effectively communicate using media. Though change is not easy, the rewards will prove to be great.

Cost and Benefit

Motivations for using media in ministry should be carefully examined. In many cases, churches do not consider the real reasons that they begin to incorporate media in their services. One unrealized motivation may be *church modeling*. Church modeling was very big in the 1990s, and churches everywhere were copying mega-churches such as Willow Creek and Saddleback. As I have interacted with houses of worship, I have encountered a number of churches that tried to model other ministries without great success. The churches being modeled stress the fact that God gave them a specific vision, and as a result their ministry grew. Many churches tried to mimic these ministries so closely that they failed to seek or discern a unique vision for their church. The projector revolution in the 1990s occurred partly because implementing media was part of the popular church model. Making sure that media is right for your church is important; it is a mistake to implement projection simply because other churches are doing it. A media ministry based on church modeling will most likely be ineffective, because there is no specific spiritual motivation to drive its success.

Another benefit of using media is the potential for *church growth*. A strong incentive for implementing media is that more people may attend a church that appears to be relevant to them. This is, of course, a desirable effect! A church that effectively applies media to its services is sure to attract new visitors. Be aware, however, that media is not merely a gimmick to bring more people through the church doors. Growth should be both physical and spiritual. Though media may increase the physical numbers, it should primarily be used as a tool to promote spiritual growth and enrichment. Balanced application of media can help you achieve both types of growth. I would personally rather attend a small church striving for spiritual maturity than a large church that is merely "a cool place to go." There is unquestionably an element of *entertainment* when using media. Some churches try to shun or ignore the entertainment factor, while others may abuse it. Media should not be used as an instrument for pure entertainment; nor should it be relegated to a mere support mechanism for church as usual. Since this can be a major point of contention, it deserves special attention. We will discuss entertainment in greater detail in Chapter 4.

Church modeling, church growth, and visual entertainment are not inherently bad motivations for incorporating media in ministry. Many valuable lessons can be learned from other churches. Physical growth is certainly not something to avoid. Entertainment can be an effective communication technique. The key to implementing an effective media ministry is *balance.* When these fundamentals are reasonably applied to a specific church situation, media will work wonders.

Having served on staff at several churches, I have noticed that new concepts tend to be introduced to a congregation either at light speed or at a snail's pace. The pendulum of change either swings too drastically or not at all. A church that goes full bore with new ideas will find that the pendulum will swing so far as to disrupt the growth of the church. It may even cause members to leave the church. Eventually the pendulum will swing back toward the middle, restoring balance, but at a high cost. Other churches introduce change so slowly that they never gain any momentum for making lasting, concrete changes. Neither scenario represents a balanced approach, yet many churches tend to repeat these patterns of implementing change.

Concerns About Starting a Media Ministry

You may have already started a media ministry of some kind in your church. If this is the case, these ideas and principles may help you focus or re-start your ministry.

Since media ministry is still a relatively new field for the church, many churches simply did the best they could—making it up as they went—without really understanding or utilizing the full potential of media. Only now are they able to see in hindsight what they *should* have done when starting a media ministry. If you find your own media ministry in a similar place, I hope that reading this book might challenge you and provide you with the opportunity to rekindle and reshape your ministry.

If, however, you are in the initial stages of considering a media ministry, you no doubt have many concerns. Implementing a media ministry—gaining congregational support, finding money to purchase equipment, and finding volunteers to do the work—can be a big step for some churches and a scary proposition. I will describe several of the main apprehensions and then offer *one word* that will dissolve these fears.

The first concern is how the addition of media will be *perceived*. What will the congregation think when a worldly device is installed in "their" sanctuary? I once was asked to explain to a general assembly in a church why their staff wanted to purchase projection equipment. A video company had set up a demonstration for that Sunday morning. I enthusiastically explained to the church the benefits of using media to expand the church's ministry. At the end of my presentation, I asked if there were any questions. Immediately an older woman stood up and said, "I'm extremely offended that you would bring the world into my sanctuary! It disgusts me!" Another member chimed in, "Is it supposed to replace our hymn books? What's next—do away with the Bible?" And another, "We need to be less like the world, not more like it! We'll lose our heritage!" Needless to say, I went from excited to terrified. Although I handled the situation with as much grace as possible, I later realized that I was battling preconceived notions about media and its effect on a traditional church. Many churches will encounter this problem. People may think that adding a media ministry is equivalent to "going Hollywood" or wanting to be like the church down the street. It may appear to be a huge compromise to some and a very frightening prospect to others. This does not have to be the case. *One word* will help to erase a congregation's apprehensions about using media in worship....

Another concern is the time and effort involved in installing a projection system. *"It's a hassle!"* Just as it is difficult to "retrofit" a traditional church with new ways to communicate, it is very often a challenge to integrate a projection system into a building that was not designed for it. It can take a considerable amount of time to determine the proper equipment and method of installation. Money can be a source of contention in many churches, and a new projection system can be a strain on any church's budget. Some churches may feel anxious about the video company that they work with, wondering if they are being taken for a ride. *One word* will make the work involved in integrating a media ministry seem effortless....

Fear of being taken advantage of by a company selling projectors leads us to the next concern: *"It's a hustle!"* During the aforementioned church-modeling period in the 1990s, video projectors were becoming affordable for many medium-sized churches. Projector manufacturers and audio/video companies quickly caught wind of the evolving church-projection market. Born from this "projector revolution" was a new marketplace. Since then, countless marketing campaigns to churches have been launched, new video companies dedicated to churches established, and specialized church divisions created within some of the larger projection manufacturers. After working on the selling side of media ministry for several years, I know that the projection and video industries see the church market as the largest vertical (niche) market, and everyone wants a piece of the pie. This is a valid concern when starting a media ministry. It is important to work with a company that has some concern for your ministry and does not merely see you as a marketing target. *One word* will help you determine whom to work with....

Once a system is in place, the next concern is that *"It's a headache!"* A media ministry introduces a whole new facet of church operations. People are needed to prepare the media and run the services. Advanced preparation time will be needed to create the material; therefore, music leaders and pastors must adjust their own preparation schedules. Equipment must be maintained and upgraded. Then there is the major fear that something will go wrong during a service, or a piece of equipment will not work come Sunday morning. *One word* will act as a mega-aspirin for this concern....

Finally, many churches may wonder, *"Where am I going to get my M&Ms?"* **M**oney and **M**anpower can be scarce commodities in many churches. It takes money to purchase the equipment and manpower to run it. *One word* will attract both....

The Answer to Potential Problems

The one thing that a media ministry must have in order to cope with these concerns is **VISION.** If there is one major problem with existing media ministries, it is the lack of a well-defined vision. The Bible says that without vision the people perish. I would paraphrase, "Without clear vision your media ministry is powerless." In many churches the media ministry is the equipment—the projector and the computer—and PowerPoint® is the driving force behind it all. Church members will quickly associate a media ministry with the equipment involved and seldom will be able to see past the surface. This lack of vision among the church staff and the congregation will bring to life all of the aforementioned concerns. The first step is to ask God for a clear vision and genuine enthusiasm for using media as an effective tool for ministry. Some church leaders and laypeople already possess this kind of vision and are well motivated. In many cases these people could be making six figures in a secular job, but would rather use their talents for the Kingdom. They usually have a knack for all things technical and a creative side to be reckoned with. As you are reading this you may be thinking, "That's me!" Whether it is you or someone else, it is crucial to have a key individual who will move the vision forward.

Once you have identified this leader, it is his or her responsibility to take this passion to the pastor and staff of the church. One major job of the pastor is to seek direction from God and then lead the church on that route. If the pastor does not fully grasp the potential of using media to equip the church and enhance the worship experience, then the media ministry will be doomed to mediocrity. It may take some time to generate the essential enthusiasm in some church leaders. Remember that this is a new language, and the world of media is a foreign country to some. However, it is vital that the pastor understand and take ownership of this vision so that it may filter through the church body.

Even if the vision for media ministry reaches the church staff level, seldom does it work its way to the congregation. This is a crucial step to resolving the concerns described above. If the congregation is only exposed to the money-raising and purchasing process of media ministry, then that is all it will mean to them. They will only see the projector as another piece of equipment and not the powerful tool it can be. To them it might as well be a copy machine hanging from the ceiling. Most people do not attend church for media or to be entertained. People go to church for spiritual reasons. For a church body to embrace media in ministry, it needs a spiritual motivation. Members must believe that media will help foster spiritual growth for themselves, their families, their church, and their community.

I highly recommend setting aside an entire Sunday to communicate your vision for media ministry to the church. During this service the pastor should express enthusiasm for this method of communication. The church should be made aware of the practical benefits of using media as well as the advantages for physical and spiritual growth. Several real-life examples of media implementation should be employed throughout the service. By using media to communicate during this service, the message should speak for itself.

To help both leadership and church members catch a vision to effectively use media, I have taken the liberty of writing a short sequel to one of Jesus' most popular parables. There is an accompanying PowerPoint presentation on the DVD to be used with this narrative.

"The Sower and the Seed" Part II

I often think about what Jesus was like. We know who Jesus was and we know a lot about His character, but what about His personality, the way He talked, His tone of voice, His inflections, His body language? These are all things that are not specified in the Bible. Throughout the years Jesus has been depicted in art and in drama and on film. Most of the time He is represented as a lofty intellectual— His words floating through the air—and in an English accent, of course. But I don't think that's the way He was....

Jesus loved to tell stories. In church lingo we call them parables, but they were stories. Jesus used them to communicate deep truths while, at the same time, relating to average, everyday people. Go back and read one of His stories again. This time, picture Jesus as a man who is passionate about the story He is telling. Maybe He picks up a stick and uses it as a prop. His voice is dramatic. He draws the people into the story and captivates them with the tale. You might even call Him entertaining. No wonder people gathered around to hear Him speak!

Jesus liked to give analogies of farm life. In this way, He related to the people and their everyday lives. So, in that spirit, I want to tell you a story based on one of Jesus' most popular analogies. You could call it "The Sower and the Seed Part II."

There were two farmers who lived in a valley. The soil there was rich and fertile. The ground almost begged for seed. Each farmer planted the same seed in his fields. Yes, it was the same seed, but each farmer used a different method of planting, cultivating, and harvesting the crops. The first farmer did some research and discovered the most effective techniques for growing a crop. Using these techniques meant that the costs were higher, additional learning was necessary, and taking a certain amount of risk was involved. The other farmer saw no need for new-fangled machines and fancy equipment. He had been using his old push plow for years and it seemed to work just fine.

When harvest time came around, both farmers yielded a crop, but the farmer who took advantage of more productive farming techniques produced far more than the farmer who refused to give up his push plow.

Here's what the parable means. The soil represents people who are ripe to receive Christ. The seed represents the unchanging message of salvation that Christ brought to us. The farmer who used outdated farming techniques represents the church that is unwilling to seek out the best methods of communicating the gospel: this will still yield some results, but not nearly as much as possible. The farmer who used modern farming methods depicts the church that learns to communicate in a way that is relevant to contemporary society. These churches connect with their community and make many disciples. This is the kind of church that we want to become....

This presentation should help you lay the basic groundwork for why your church should start a media ministry.

By the end of this special service, the congregation should be well motivated. Be sure to set some goals before the church body, including financial goals and building a team of workers. When the members of your church understand the spiritual motivations for using media, the major fears and objections about starting a media ministry will be quieted. There will likely be fewer *misperceptions* because the underlying motivations were explained. There will be less *hassle* because people will be excited about contributing to the fundraising and design process of the projection system. Finding a video company that understands your vision for a media ministry will help eliminate the *hustle* involved in purchasing. Your *headache* will be cured by the dozens of church members who are eager to give of their talents and be trained to support your media ministry. And the media ministry's appetite for *M&Ms* will be satisfied as the church body gives of its time and money to support a ministry it knows will ultimately benefit the Kingdom.

Chapter 2

Media Ministry Involves Gear

Designing a Media System

As we discussed in **Chapter 1**, the concern about purchasing the equipment needed to implement a media ministry can often overshadow the spiritual benefits of using this method of communication. This is a natural reaction, because this type of ministry requires specialized tools to carry it out. The "gear" involved is a major factor in a media ministry and can ultimately influence the effectiveness of the ministry. It is important to know what tools will be needed to establish and grow a successful media ministry.

Establishing your vision for media ministry is an important first step in the design and purchasing process. I suggest that you develop and document your goals in a *vision statement*, so that this statement can be a guide for the development of the media ministry, both regarding spiritual goals and equipment needs. Vision statements often begin with a basic statement summarizing the ministry in a few sentences and then move to a more detailed section that that resembles a business plan. This plan should outline some specific objectives, deadlines to meet those goals, and the equipment needed for the tasks. An example of a vision statement might be: "Our ministry would like to produce video content such as testimonials, interviews, metaphors, and other material. Using video we will be able to enhance, support, and sometimes carry the message that is delivered. We will need a computer capable of editing video, a video camera, lights, and some audio equipment. We would like to have this system in place by August of 2004." Each facet of the media ministry should be detailed in the plan. The first draft may only contain general information, but can be augmented as more details become available.

Equipment Needed: The Basics

Since equipment should be selected based on your needs, we will explore the most basic methods of using media in ministry. The first application most churches consider is the ability to project song lyrics, which is a great way to introduce media to your church. Other basic applications include projecting announcements and sermon notes, and using video clips for illustrations. The

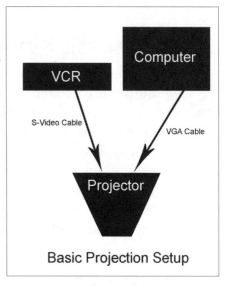

Basic Projection Setup

basic equipment required to accomplish these tasks includes a video projector, screen, computer, VCR, and all of the necessary cabling and installation hardware. From the computer to the screen, each piece of equipment is an important link in a projection system. The overall quality can be drastically affected if any of these components are substandard to the others. We will discuss factors to consider when purchasing each of these components, starting with the computer and working our way toward the screen.

The Computer

Many churches devote most of their time and money to the projector without giving much consideration to the computer, which is the source of the images being projected. Although a vital link in the chain, the projector may be equated to the "eyes" of the system, while the computer is its "heart." The temptation may be to upgrade the church secretary's computer and move their old one to the sanctuary, but that would be a major mistake. The computer needs to be a near top-of-the-line model with plenty of horsepower, dedicated solely to the media ministry. Here are several key factors to consider:

Macintosh or PC? My personal recommendation is to buy a PC-based system. I have no bias against the Macintosh computer. In fact, Macintosh systems have been advanced in the area of media and graphics for years. However, according to an informal, ongoing survey at ChurchMedia.net, 90 to 95 percent of all churches using media in ministry are PC-based. This also concurs with our visitor statistics at ChurchMedia.net and polls at my seminars. Most churches use PC systems because of their general popularity, lower costs, and the vast amount of software available for the Windows platform. Today, Windows-based systems can contend on every level with a Macintosh system. The Windows XP platform, in particular, is enhanced for working with media, and a multitude of media software and hardware is available for the PC. But in the end, it comes down to personal preference, since either type of computer will do a good job.

Laptop or Desktop? In general, a desktop computer is a better value than a laptop. Desktops have more flexibility in design choices and can usually be loaded to the teeth for less money than a laptop. The only obvious benefit to a laptop is its portability. If this is a major factor, the good news is that laptops have recently made strides in the area of graphics power. It is now possible to buy an adequate laptop for less than $2,000.

The Graphics Card/Chip. This is arguably the most important component in a computer designed for media. Since the graphics card connects to the projector's computer (or data) input, an inadequate card will act as a bottleneck in the whole system. Graphics cards have their very own memory (RAM) on board. Having lots of memory gives the card plenty of breathing space for quickly displaying graphics and animations. A card with at least 32 megabytes (MB) of RAM is recommended. Other specifications to look for include 3-D acceleration and MPEG-2 (DVD) decoding. Dual graphics cards are suggested and are explained in more detail in **Section 3** of this book. We can thank the video game industry for driving the quality level of graphics cards, which has in turn improved the quality of cards included in basic computer configurations.

System RAM. System RAM (*random access memory*) refers to the main computer system memory. Like graphics RAM, system RAM gives the computer the headroom needed to quickly accomplish tasks. Operating much like our short-term memory, the RAM keeps the operating system, applications, and data being worked open so that the processor can quickly reach them. The more RAM you have, the more information can be held in short-term memory and the faster this information can be accessed. The current price of RAM is very affordable, so you should get as much as you can possibly afford (or will fit in your system). I recommend that your system is equipped with at least 512 MB of system RAM.

Processor Speed. Believe it or not, the processor speed of a computer gets more attention than it deserves. While it is important, its benefits are mainly only noticed when serious number-crunching is involved. A faster processor will be of great benefit for editing video, 3-D animations, or very large graphics files. Though less crucial than you might think, having a higher processor speed does enhance performance. I recommend an *Intel*® Pentium III or IV processor with a speed of 1.3 GB or higher. *Celeron* chips should be avoided. Though *AMD* chips are fine, I have found the Intel chips to be a bit more stable, especially when editing video.

Hard Drives. There are two considerations when choosing a hard drive: size and speed. For graphics-only applications, 30 GB or larger is recommended and speed is not as crucial. But for working with audio and video, these specifications become more important. Hard drive recommendations for audio/video are detailed in **Section 4** of this book.

Motherboard. The motherboard hosts or connects all of the components in a computer and helps them communicate with each other. The speed at which the components speak to each other (bus speed) is determined by the motherboard. The type of motherboard also usually dictates the type of processor and RAM to be used. There are also upgrade considerations when investigating motherboard specifications. You will want to determine if the motherboard can be upgraded with more RAM, a second video card, and a video-editing card. Consult with a qualified computer expert to decide which motherboard is right for your application.

Projectors

The projector quickly becomes the focus (no pun intended) of most media ministries, and is usually the most expensive component. Projection technology continues to improve with each passing year. Projectors are becoming lighter, brighter, and more affordable. Here are some basic considerations when shopping for a projector:

Brightness. The biggest challenge that most churches will encounter with using a projector has to do with interference from the existing light situation in the area where it is used. In many cases, an abundant amount of light is already present from windows and any stage lighting. Although there are several techniques for minimizing this problem, the most obvious solution would be to employ a high-brightness projector. The brightness of a projector is measured in ANSI lumens. There is no magical number of ANSI lumens that will solve any lighting problem. The appropriate number of ANSI lumens needed will vary greatly from church to church. As with most things technical, more is usually better. Projectors equipped with 2,000 or more ANSI lumens have become affordable enough for many churches.

Resolution. Resolution measures image quality and size. Projectors have a *native* resolution, which is its true resolution. Many projectors on the market today have a native resolution of 800 x 600 (or SVGA). While these projectors may handle higher resolutions such as 1024 x 768 (XGA), they will compress a larger image area to fit into their native format. In most church applications, a native resolution of SVGA or XGA is sufficient. More detailed information about resolution will be covered in **Section 2**.

Contrast Ratio. The contrast ratio represents the difference between the brightest and the darkest portions of an image. Higher contrast ratios will usually yield a more colorful, detailed picture. Most projectors available today have more than adequate contrast ratios of up to 350:1 and higher.

Exchangeable Lenses. Many projectors come with only one lens option, though some situations may require a different lens. Various lenses are designed to focus and zoom at certain distances from the screen. The projector lens will not focus or size the image appropriately if it is out of its focus/zoom range. In these cases, a different lens must be installed in the projector. For example, a long-throw lens may be necessary when installing a projector at the back of a room. A short-throw lens may be needed when using rear projection. If you do find that the standard lens will not work, the first and most desirable option would be to get an optional lens directly from the manufacturer. If one is not available, it is sometimes possible to find an after-market lens for the specific situation. Keep in mind that changing the lens will usually change the brightness of the projector as well. If there are no available lenses, the only option would be to explore other projector models. Make sure you understand the "throw distance" specifications of the projector you are considering and make sure that it will focus and zoom from the location where you plan to install the projector.

Input Connections. Current model projectors have standard computer and video connections. The **computer input** (sometimes called the **data input**) is a 15-pin connector, which looks like the end of a monitor cable but is female. There are one or two of these inputs on the projector. The computer's graphics card output is connected to the projector's computer input with basically a very long monitor cable.

The second standard input on a projector is the **video input**. A VCR may be connected to the projector via the familiar RCA-type input (composite) or an s-video input. Using s-video will yield better results. Naturally, a VCR with an s-video output is required to use this connection. Most S-VHS VCRs on the market feature an s-video output and can be obtained for less than $200.

Finally, some projectors have a **component input**. The term "component" is sometimes referred to as "RGB-5." Using this type of connection will result in the best overall picture quality. A component input separates a video signal in up to five parts: red, blue, green, horizontal sync, and vertical sync. To use this input, the graphics and video signals need to be converted at the sending end using a special piece of equipment or sometimes using a simple cable adapter. Once converted, the signal is sent over five cables, usually bundled together, and into the five corresponding connectors on the projector. This method is usually more expensive, since conversion equipment is needed, and the cable costs more. But the resulting difference in quality is well worth it.

Running Cables and Amplifiers

At minimum, two of the following types of cable need to be run from the media control area to the projector: a computer (15-pin or component) and a video (composite or S-video) cable. For longer cables over seventy-five feet it may be necessary to add a signal amplifier at the sending end of the cable to help boost the signal. Remote control cables for the projector and screen may also be installed at the same time. In many cases the cables may be run through a conduit, which is basically a pipe inside a wall, under a floor or above a ceiling. The size of conduit installed for cables should be big enough for additional cables to be added later if the system is expanded.

Screens

The final destination of the image is, of course, the screen. It is important to understand that a screen is needed in every projection system: a wall should *never* be used as a substitute. Screens reflect back light and are designed to give an accurate representation of the colors in an image. (Walls are for paint and wallpaper!)

Front or Rear Projection? Because it is generally accepted that projecting from the behind a screen results in a better image, you should first determine if rear projection is possible. In many cases rear projection will not be possible because of structural limitations since a room dedicated to the projector needs to be located behind the screen. Most churches will not be able to accommodate rear projection because of this requirement. If, however, rear-screen projection is possible, mirror systems can be obtained that will reduce the amount of throw distance (distance from the projector to the screen) needed, thus reducing the size of the room. When building a new church, rear projection needs to be considered in the early stages of design.

Types of Screens. If rear projection is not possible, you will need to determine the most suitable type of front projection screen. Many churches opt for a motorized, retractable screen that can be put out of sight when not in use. Another option, a permanently tensioned screen, simply attaches to a wall and will always be visible. In either case, a front projection screen can be built into the existing church décor. With a little imagination and the talent of a carpenter, screens can often blend in and add to the ambiance of an auditorium. If you are a "church on the go," then there are also several portable screen types to choose from.

Screen Surfaces. Without going into great detail, both front and rear projection configurations come with several different surface options. The most common type of front projection surface is matte white and has a reflection gain of 1:1, meaning that it reflects back the same amount of light that it receives. A *high gain* screen will actually amplify the light that it receives, but has a much narrower viewing cone, meaning that you cannot see the image as well as you move away from the center of the screen. A high gain screen works well in churches that are not incredibly wide.

Screen Placement. The placement of the screen is a crucial consideration. The screen (or screens) needs to be installed in an area where there are no line-of-sight problems and where it does not take up stage space. The screen should be located in a dark area so there is little or no light hitting the screen except for the projector image. Stage lights should be directed away from the screen.

Screen Size. The basic calculation used to determine screen size involves measuring the distance from the row of seats farthest from the screen and dividing by six. This will roughly give you the width of the screen needed. Standard screens sizes are 6 x 8, 9 x 12, and 12 x 14. The ratio of the width and height of these screen sizes is 4:3. There is slightly more width than height. Currently, this is the standard screen aspect ratio. However, in the near future, all screens will be a 16:9 aspect ratio or widescreen format. See **Appendix A** for more information on the widescreen format and its benefits to a church.

System Design: Beyond the Basics

After purchasing a standard projection system, I have found that many churches discover certain limitations of their setup. Many of these drawbacks manifest themselves as distractions during a service. Here's a typical scenario. The song service has just finished and it's time to switch the projector's input so you can show that wonderful video that took you all night to finish. The congregation sits in silent anticipation. You grab the remote and press "Video 1." The blue screen of death flashes up with the words *Video Input 1*, and *Play* from the VCR. The mood set by the worship team has been broken (or at least interrupted) by the very devices that helped create the atmosphere in the first place. To make things worse, the video image is dark and the colors are dingy.

Limiting distractions during worship should be a prime consideration when using media in the church. Exposed computer programs, blue screens, and onscreen displays should be avoided at all costs. Media ministers worldwide dream of seamless switching, and even fading, between computer and video sources. Many do not know what equipment is necessary to provide a distraction-free environment. However, several manufacturers have developed products to provide solutions to these vexing distractions.

Below we'll consider each of these problems and offer a solution.

Problem: *When I show videos, the image is dark and dingy.*

Solution: *Scale up or double the video signal.*

A projector's native "habitat" is high-resolution. The technology that a projector uses to display images is at the same resolution level as a computer monitor. Many make the mistake of assuming that a projector is more like a television, but they are very different types of display devices. A standard video signal from a VCR is roughly half the *scan rate* of a computer signal (the output from a graphics card). In order for a projector to display a video signal at a higher resolution, the signal needs to be stepped up, or *scaled*, which will maximize the image quality capabilities of the projector. Devices known as *scalers* and *scan-line doublers* will take a composite or s-video signal from a video source and convert it to a high-resolution, VGA signal. The output from a scaler is usually a 15-pin connector (like a VGA cable), though some have component outputs, which are more desirable. Keep in mind that the projector must also have component inputs if the scaler has a component output. In either case, only ONE cable run to the projector is required.

Problem: *I want to SWITCH between computer and video quickly and without any distractions.*

Best Solution: *Use a scaler or doubler with multiple inputs and switching capabilities.*

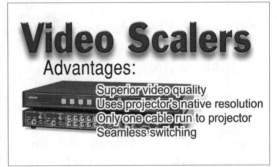

Some scalers and doublers include several video inputs and a computer input, which are switchable via buttons on the front of the unit. In a church application, an operator could perform a "hard" switch (or cut) between a PowerPoint slide and a video clip on a VCR by simply pressing the corresponding input button. Depending on the capabilities of the equipment, there may be a slight flicker when switching.

Budget Solution: *Use a simple converter and switcher.*

If scalers are out of reach financially, several converters are available. These products do not increase the resolution of the video, but merely convert the signal into a type that can be displayed though a projector's computer input. The output of this converter is a standard VGA connector.

This output and the output from the graphics card of a computer may be connected to a standard VGA monitor switcher, allowing an operator to quickly switch between video and computer. Again, only one cable run to the projector is needed in this situation.

Problem: *I want to MIX or cross-fade between computer and video.*

Best Solution: *Dig deep and use a high-resolution mixer.*

Scalers and doublers with switching capabilities have been available for some time. Recently, several companies have released products with the ability to *mix* video and computer signals at the high-resolution level, allowing for cross-fades and other effects between a video and computer source. This would allow a media operator to seamlessly fade from a PowerPoint slide to a video clip on a VCR. A dream come true? That depends on your budget! Since these products are fairly new and still developing, the cost of the equipment may be out of range for some churches.

Budget Solution: *Lower the resolution of your computer signal and use a standard video mixer.*

If mixing computer and video is a feature that is a must-have but also a can't-afford, a less expensive solution would be to use a scan-converter and video mixer. Scan-converters are available at many different quality levels. The price usually is indicative of the quality.

A scan-converter will lower the resolution of a computer signal to match that of a video signal. The output of the scan-converter can then be fed into a video mixer along with other video signals. However, this solution should be avoided unless absolutely necessary. When a scan-converter is introduced into a projection system there *is* a noticeable loss in image quality. I highly recommend avoiding scan converters if at all possible. Remember that projectors are more like computer monitors than televisions, and they prefer a high-resolution signal.

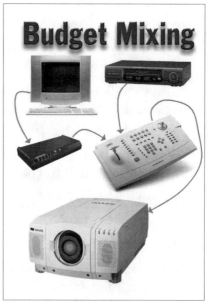

Problem: *My VCR displays* **Play** *and* **Stop** *and shows an ugly blue screen.*

Solution: *Use a different VCR or master cueing and switching.*

The easiest way to avoid on-screen displays is to use a VCR with the ability to switch that feature off. Refer to the VCR manual or explore the menu functions to find out if a VCR has this ability. As a general rule of thumb, a VCR with an s-video connector will most likely allow the on-screen display to be switched off. Since using s-video is more desirable that a standard composite signal anyway, the advantages of purchasing a new VCR with s-video capabilities would be well worthwhile. These VCRs also will usually display a black screen instead of blue when no video input signal is detected.

If you *must* use a VCR that doesn't have the option to switch off its onscreen display, another solution would be to learn how to cue videos and master timing when switching. For instance, if the word *Play* appears for five seconds, cue the video to five seconds before the beginning of the clip to be shown. When the onscreen display disappears, switch to the video source. Keep in mind that you will need a video monitor for this. Also realize that if there is audio during the five-second lag, it will need to be muted during that time. To avoid seeing the word *Stop*, simply switch back to the computer signal before pressing *Stop* on the VCR.

IMAG

A colleague of mine was throwing around the word IMAG during a conference call with several other media "gurus." I had no idea what he was talking about. Embarrassed to ask, I did some research and finally found out that IMAG stands for **I**mage **MAG**nification. It basically means live video. I had never encountered the term because I rarely work with a church that is large enough to need to display live video on the sanctuary screen. Live video should only be used by churches with auditoriums so large that it is difficult to see the people on the stage. IMAG should not be implemented "just for fun" or because the church down the street is doing it. There is no room for error when using cameras for live video. Smaller churches that do not need IMAG support will find it to be more of a distraction than a benefit. This does not necessarily mean that a media ministry should not employ two or three cameras to tape a service; it just means that the material being recorded does not need to be seen on the big screen.

Purchasing Equipment

Hire a Consultant!

Although we have covered the basics of system design, we have really only scratched the surface. Unforeseen challenges are often encountered when installing a projection system. If possible, these challenges need to be identified before determining a budget and the specific equipment needed. Because a certain amount of expertise is required to recognize potential problems, hiring a *consultant* who specializes in projection systems for churches is prudent. Unfortunately, most churches skip this essential step in the design process.

Churches that have not sought outside help in the area of technology have already paid dearly. For example, during the past fifty years, churches have become dependent on sound reinforcement as a means of amplifying the spoken word and, more recently, for supporting praise bands with a full complement of instruments and vocalists. As new churches have been built and older churches modified, proper audio design has largely been neglected. Church leaders have relied too much on second-hand information or have not sought any audio consultation at all. As a result, a multitude of poorly designed worship auditoriums with inadequate audio systems *still* exist. These mistakes are usually costly in more ways than one. Not only is money wasted on insufficient equipment, poor building design is usually irreparable. The cost of bringing in an expert will usually be offset by the money and headache that will be saved by making proper decisions from the beginning.

For instance, I once visited a church that was starting a media ministry. The company they had been working with had recommended that a small projector be placed on the floor at the front of the auditorium and projected onto a screen that would take up most of the stage space. The room was rather small but had a high ceiling. I wondered why the company had not suggested shooting the image from the back of the room onto a screen above the stage. "They told us we could not afford to do that," was the response. After having the bid reworked, the church was able to purchase a system that was within the budget and that worked better for their particular setting. Hiring an independent consultant is always a good idea, since he or she will likely have knowledge of a wider range of options and products. There is also less likely to be a conflict of interest when the company selling the product is not also making the recommendations for installation.

When designing a new building, it is crucial to bring in an audio/video consultant very early in the process. I have heard countless stories of how an architect designed a new auditorium without seriously considering the audio and video needs. In such cases, a great deal of friction generally occurs when the A/V consultant is finally contacted because of the many changes that need to be made to accommodate the audio and video equipment. In the worst cases, the building may already be under construction when the A/V consultant is hired. To avoid these situations, a consultant should be contacted before or at the same time as the architect. Though style and aesthetics have traditionally been the paramount consideration when constructing a church building, audio and video requirements are at least equal in importance for churches seeking to use media as a prime means of communication.

Shop, Shop, Shop!

After a consultant has provided the proper guidance, it is then time to pull out the checkbook. There are three types of shopping that should be considered. The first is *price shopping*. Pricing for electronics is extremely competitive, especially in the area of video. The team members in charge of purchasing should make sure they have done their research and are getting a great price on the equipment needed.

Price is not always the prime consideration, however. A church should also *service* shop. Sometimes it is worthwhile to buy from a company that charges more but offers more valuable services.

Important questions to ask about any company you are considering are:

- Do they install the equipment?

- If so, do they warranty their work?

- If the projector breaks, will they take care of the warranty procedure?

- Will they offer a loaner or rental while the projector is being repaired?

- Are they available for assistance on weekends?

Finally, a church should *knowledge* shop. During my time in the projector business, I quickly learned that there are more salesmen than qualified experts in the field of "display technology." It is very important to work with a company that is not just interested in selling something, but rather in selling the right equipment for the church's situation. Some salespeople may tell a buyer what they want to hear in order to make a sale. It is a good idea to test the salesperson. Find out the answer to a fairly complicated technical question and ask the salesperson the question. If he or she gives an incorrect answer, find another company to work with. If the salesperson gives a correct answer or says, "I don't know, but I'll find out," then that should be a good company to deal with.

Demonstrating the Equipment

Once an A/V company has been selected, arrange for a four-week demo of the equipment. Often the company will rent the equipment and allow the church to apply the rental fee toward a purchase. Using the equipment for four weeks in a row will give the church a chance to become acclimated to media and to see the benefits. The four services should be well planned and show various ways that media can be used in ministry. At the end of the demo period, remove the equipment and put the old overhead projector back in place. The church will immediately see the difference and dig deep to help pay for the new system as soon as possible. This technique is a great motivator to start a fundraising program for the system.

Most churches make extra efforts to raise the initial chunk of money required to install a projection system, but fail to see the need for future funding of a media ministry. There will be software upgrades, projector bulbs, new technologies and better equipment to consider for future purchasing. Therefore, it is important to start a media ministry budget. Many times the media budget is lumped in with the music ministry line item. The media ministry needs its own line item even if it is small to begin with. This will give the media department more validity and its own identity. It will also give those in charge of finances an idea of how much money is involved in growing a media ministry.

Don't Be a Gear Junkie

"Hello, my name is Tim Eason, and I'm a gear junkie." It's true, I love buying and playing with all things electronic. While I'm willing to admit my addiction, I've learned some valuable lessons to pass on to other gear junkies. Back in the early 1990s I desperately wanted to be the next Michael W. Smith. I was a keyboard player and during those days the keyboard revolution was in full swing. Keyboards were obsolete literally *before* they hit the market. At the time I worked at a pro music shop just so I could buy equipment at wholesale. I bought keyboards and sold them for pennies on the dollar so I could always have the latest and the greatest. There came a time, however, when I just could not afford to keep upgrading. With my credit maxed out, I had to sit down and just work with what I had. Ironically, during that period I produced the best material of my short-lived music career!

Media ministers who are gear junkies may fall into the same rut, always feeling that they need more equipment or better software to do their job. Throughout this book I discuss various levels of gear that can be used, while keeping in mind that most churches do not have a large budget. Though I often challenge churches to spend more on media ministry, I am constantly amazed at what people can accomplish with what would be considered primitive software and equipment. The key to getting the most out of the resources available to a church is *stewardship.* I honestly feel that if a church uses what it has to the best of its ability, God will bless its efforts and provide better resources in time. A media ministry that actively uses what is available will be far more effective than a media ministry that is dormant because the church feels that it does not have the proper equipment.

Chapter 3

Building a Strong Media Team

Acquiring the appropriate equipment needed to reach your vision of a media ministry represents only part of the bigger picture. If media is seen as an art form and the equipment likened to brushes and paint, then the quality of the art will lie in the hands of the artists. Many churches may rely on only *one* such media artist to generate creative media content. Putting this responsibility on the shoulders of one or two people will usually result in media that continually has the same flavor. Both the congregation and the artists themselves may burn out unless the workload can be distributed. To avoid this potential problem a church should assemble *two* media ministry teams, each with a distinct function—a *vision team* and an *action team*.

The Vision Team

The vision team should consist of at least five types of people. As we discuss each member, try to think of someone in your church that best fits the description. Write down his or her name, and by the end of this section you will have the list of your vision team members!

The best person to lead this team will be the *media minister* or person with the most passion for using media in ministry. We described this person in Chapter 1 when explaining the process of taking the vision to the church. To recap, the leader of the vision team usually has a great deal of technical and/or creative talent and is convinced that using media is the best way to communicate God's Word. There has been some mild debate about what title to assign this person.[1] Some argue that calling this person a "Media Minister" or "Media Pastor" borders on heresy. Personally, I think it depends on the person's calling. If the person sees his or her role as merely technical support, then a ministerial title probably isn't appropriate. I would also suggest that having a serious passion for using media to further the Kingdom of God is a necessary qualification for a team leader. Having traveled the country and conversed with countless people in the field, I have found that genuine media ministers are those who feel a literal call from God to work in this area of ministry.

I personally can attest to the legitimacy of the term "Media Minister." I have always known that I would be involved in full-time church work. I delivered my first sermon at age six in my family's living room. With a TV tray as a pulpit, I held a service complete with music and even multimedia (puppets). At the time, I think I just wanted to be like my Dad, but the desire to work in church never left me. Throughout the years I explored every possibility of ministerial work and at different times of my life I wanted to be a pastor, music minister, missionary, Christian counselor, and even a Christian rock star! When none of these areas of ministry seemed to gel for me, I became discouraged. Growing up I also had been developing a talent for things of a technical nature. I assumed that these skills in computers, graphics, and video only amounted to hobbies that would distract me from the rigors of church work. Then, during the 1990s when media started to become more prevalent in churches, it became obvious that God had been preparing me for the *media ministry*. Then my life came into focus and started to make sense. (After serving as a media minister for a time I felt another call to equip other churches. It was then that I became one of the first "media missionaries.") I have heard similar stories from numerous media ministers throughout the country.

Once you have identified your leader, you should consider hiring her or him as part of your church staff.[2] With the majority of the media support relegated to a volunteer base, the amount of time dedicated to the implementation of media may be limited and adversely affect the quality and effectiveness of a media ministry. Though it is not realistic to expect most churches to hire several people dedicated to media ministry, any church serious about media should hire at least one person to head up this area. This may be a full- or part-time hourly position or salaried. The media minister leads both the vision and the action teams. Media ministers coordinate and train the volunteers, make creative decisions, and manage the equipment involved. They are also heavily involved in supporting or driving every aspect of a worship service, from the music to the sermon.

A common question is how much a media minister should be paid. Because of dramatic variations in church budgets, no standard salary can be suggested. The important thing to remember is that people involved in media are worth a great deal of money in the secular field. They should be paid as much as possible and given adequate benefits. The title of "Media Minister" is fairly new and a growing position. Some church bodies may have a hard time accepting this as a ministerial job and question the importance and value of the position. Again, bringing the vision to the church will help with this potential dilemma when hiring a media minister. In the world of media, formal education is not as crucial as talent, experience, and commitment. While some seminaries have begun to recognize this new calling, it is still difficult to find a course of study in the area of media ministry. Formal education, whether secular or from a religious institution, is desirable, but should not be the main factor in hiring a media minister or in determining her or his salary level.

Even if the media minister is on staff, the next person to recruit for the vision team is a *senior staff member*. Having another staff member on the team will ensure that the vision of the media ministry is in constant sync with the overall vision of the church. With two staff members on the team there will be less confusion, better communication, and more accountability. Usually this person will be the senior pastor or music minister.

Next on the list of vision team members will be someone with a *creative mind*. I've always said that there is a fine line between being creative and being deranged. Every church has this type of person in their midst. These creative persons are usually full of energy and often involved in drama. The creativity and wealth of ideas flowing from these people make them an invaluable part of the vision team. They also help add excitement and energy to the media ministry.

A *technical person* will also be needed to help bring creative ideas to fruition. For instance, when the creative person dreams up a grandiose concept for a Christmas production full of video and lighting effects, the technical person can let the team know what is necessary to accomplish the task. A person who is very familiar with the technical arts will make sure that the direction that the media ministry takes is realistic and can be accomplished with the tools available to that church. This team member can act as a ground wire (pun intended) for the vision team and provide invaluable insight into what a media ministry can achieve.

So far we have identified four people for the vision team: the media minister, staff member, creative mind, and technical person. Even if you happen to find one person who possesses all of these attributes, the vision team still needs to have several people. Even the most talented of media ministers needs others to help generate ideas and keep the ministry fresh and dynamic.

The final vision team member is often overlooked. When a church first considers a media ministry, many times there is an unspoken fear of the senior members in the church. Pastoral staff may think, "If anyone is going to object to this new technology it will be our older members." While we have already discussed ways to circumvent misperceptions, the temptation may be to ignore the senior crowd and deal with problems as they arise. An effective way to communicate the vision of the media ministry to the older congregation is to include a *senior member* on the vision team. Find a person who understands the vision of the media ministry and can act as a liaison with his or her peers. This team member is crucial to any church with an established older congregation. By including them in the vision of the media ministry, many seniors will surprise a church with unexpected enthusiasm and support. See **Appendix B**, "No Room for Traditional Worship Anymore?"

Developing the Vision

Once the vision team members are in place, they should begin to develop the higher-level, more cerebral and spiritual elements of the media ministry. The initial mission for this team will be to formulate a vision statement for the media ministry. As we have already noted several times, the vision of this ministry will drive everything from purchasing to implementation. Therefore, this team should be assembled and establish a plan before any action is taken.

Once the vision is solidified, it is very important to stick to that plan. During the mid-1990s when vision statements were becoming more prevalent in churches, every department in my church was asked to develop a vision statement (except, ironically, the media department). Each minister prayed earnestly for specific goals and carefully crafted a finely tuned vision statement, sometimes agonizing over the choice of a single word in a phrase. The vision statements were then presented to the church body during a special service. They seemed to signal a new beginning for the church, and the air was filled with anticipation of great things to come. A year went by, and while some of the short-term goals of the church were met, most of the aspirations and objectives put forth in the vision statements disappeared, never to be realized. The reason for this unfortunate outcome is simple to explain and fairly common among churches. The church experienced a short period of vision and motivation, only to fall back into the rhetoric of "doing church." All of the things that have to be done in order to run a church and conduct worship took precedence and eventually snuffed out the vision.

To help keep the vision of the media ministry alive, the vision team should gather regularly for *vision-check meetings* every four to six weeks. Those who wear glasses know that they must return to an eye doctor on a regular basis because their eyes may continue to grow out of focus. Similarly, the vision team should get together to make sure that the vision of the media ministry is still in focus and has not veered from its original course. The team may also discover that the media ministry vision may need a new "prescription." Regular meetings therefore provide an opportunity to adjust the vision if necessary. If part of the original plan is not working, then it is best to explore other avenues. A certain amount of experimentation will be part of the growth process; however, any changes should be well planned and not executed frivolously. Too much experimentation can be detrimental to many congregations.

The Action Team

Once the vision team is in place, you will want to begin assembling the *action team* next. The action team does the "grunt" work of producing the media and running the equipment during the service. If a church wonders where to get people for this team, one only needs to look out into the congregation on a Sunday morning. Media ministry is fun; you will no doubt find dozens of people who would love to be on the team.

An Effective Team Begins With the Coach

As with any group, the person in charge can make or break the team. It is essential that a media minister not only have technical and creative skill, but also possess the qualities of a good leader. In high school I was a member of a championship football team...a *flag football* team. I played in a Christian league for the school that I attended, and we were undefeated for two years in a row. Our team, the "Son-Blazers," was the team to beat! This wasn't always the case, however. In our first year, the team won only one game during the whole season. We were terrible! The following year the school hired a new coach, Coach Cline, who proved to be a tough coach. He trained us like a regular tackle-football team. Our calisthenics program was rigorous; I've never been in better physical shape since. But Coach Cline knew that being physically fit was only half the training. He also concentrated on building us into a working unit and increasing our self-esteem. He may have been handed a losing team, but he saw winners in all of us.

One boy on the team couldn't throw or catch and did not seem to be a natural athlete. The ball would bounce off his chest every time. He seemed hopeless. Though he tried to quit the team several times, Coach Cline wouldn't let him. This kid did have one talent: he could outrun anyone on the team and would have made a great receiver...if he could only catch. Rather than giving up on him, Coach Cline decided to capitalize on the boy's speed. If he could develop this kid's ability to pull flags from the opposing team, he would be a valuable asset. The coach ran special drills just for the boy, and his skill at capturing flags eventually matched his talent for speed. He became a star defensive lineman in the league and was a formidable opponent to any offense attempting to cross the goal line. Coach Cline could have easily said, "This kid isn't made for sports," and let him go. I was that kid. Coach Cline had the vision to work with my skills and develop me into a valuable athlete. If he had not, I never would have played on a championship football team. I would not have tasted victory as a result of hard work. I learned that every member of the team is extremely important, even if his position is not as glamorous as others. Most of all, I base my fundamental principles for building a media ministry team on this foundational team experience.

The leader, or "coach," of a media team needs to have the vision to see beyond the surface and the ability to recognize potential team members. For example, let's suppose that someone enthusiastically approaches the media minister after a service about the presentation software used during worship. He asks, "What do you do for a living?" She says, "I'm a housewife with a ton of time on my hands. I'm into decorating, but I don't know a thing about computers." That's when he introduces her to the "CompuGeek"[3] on the team. The CompuGeek is a great whiz kid who speaks in acronyms and knows everything about computers. By combining their gifts and talents, these two very different people become valuable team members. The housewife has an eye for design and color, while the CompuGeek knows the ins and outs of the software. If the CompuGeek teaches the housewife how to operate the software, then the media ministry now has an extremely powerful team member!

The success of that flag football team exemplifies the importance of quality leadership. All team members—even those whose talents seem less suited to the task—can become potential champions in the hands of an effective leader. Remember that a media minister leads one of the most visual and crucial aspects of a worship service. He or she should be a strong and compassionate leader, able to see the potential in team members and help them develop their natural skills. In time, any group can become a championship team!

Train Them Up

With this concept in mind, find willing volunteers and train them. In addition to one-on-one guidance, a regularly scheduled training day every four to six weeks will keep the team sharp. There is nothing more detrimental to a media ministry than complacency. Continual training will challenge the team to constantly strive for a higher level of quality. There are several good magazines dedicated to church technology, such as *Church Production* and *Technologies for Worship*. (See **Appendix D** for additional resources.) Each team member should receive a copy. There are also a number of church technology conferences and training workshops held throughout the country. Many of these workshops may be integrated into larger conferences about a related topic such as music ministry. The National Religious Broadcasters association has recently added sessions dedicated to in-house media ministry. Sometimes audio/video companies will sponsor workshops to help promote their company. While these types of workshops are not held on a regular basis, there are several training events that occur each year (See **Appendix E**). These events provide great opportunities to equip a media team and network with other media ministries.

Because 99 percent of the equipment and software that churches use in their media ministry was not designed specifically for church use, there are also countless secular resources for training. While technical training with a church slant is more desirable, other opportunities for education should not be ignored. A listing of helpful magazines and training events not specifically related to church work can be found in **Appendix F**.

Make It an EVENT!

Creating an atmosphere of excitement surrounding the media ministry will not only help attract volunteers for the action team, but will also help create team cohesiveness.

As with any recruiting process, better results will be achieved when the task is presented less like work and more like play. You might try giving the team a clever name relating to technology in ministry. Matching shirts with the team name on them will help unify the team and identify them as valuable contributors to a worship service. Team members who show hard work and dedication should occasionally be recognized. All members should be constantly encouraged. The team should sometimes get together just to get to know one another and share common interests. Creating a fun and rewarding environment will promote commitment and diligence within an action team.

Recruit Youth

Youth are a natural goldmine for media ministry. Young people often have more time to dedicate to the ministry, and a natural enthusiasm and talent for working with computers. They also are apt to catch on to new technology very quickly. A marketing director for a company that produces video editing equipment told me that it takes two hours for an adult to teach another adult how to use their product. He went on to say that it takes thirty minutes for a young person to teach another young person the same thing. Having grown up in a technological environment, this type of work is second nature for many youth. While youth definitely need some supervision when using equipment, adults should not be overly cautious or hesitant to let younger team members handle expensive gear. Heavily involving youth in the media ministry gives them an important role to play in the life of the church. This will create strong church members, future church leaders, and perhaps future media ministers. As with prospecting in any goldmine, some digging may be needed to find the genuine article, but the time and effort involved will pay off in the long run.

Dealing with Difficult Team Members

Inevitably a media ministry team will have to deal with difficult interpersonal issues. Sometimes a team member may lose sight of the fact that he or she is participating in a ministry team, and let his or her ego and pride get in the way. This may manifest itself as a desire to control things, which can cause disruption not only among team members, but also getting the work accomplished. Ultimately this can affect every part of a worship service because that person may be a spiritual drag on the worship team and church staff. Many times leaders may be reluctant to address this situation, especially if the person causing the problems has been in a position for a long time. No matter how painful, the situation needs to be discussed with the person in a loving way, and an effort made to improve the situation. If things do not improve and a person continues to be a disruption, then it may be necessary to ask the person to take a break from the team. In essence, the team member should be "benched," strengthened, and then put back on the field—just as any good coach would do.

Techies Need Food Too

One way to ensure that the team is spiritually on track is to turn the action team into a small group. Oftentimes the spiritual life of those who are heavily involved in preparing and supporting worship services may inadvertently be neglected. Being caught up in the mechanics of running the technical side of a church service can frequently interfere with a team member's ability to plug in to other areas of church life. This may be overlooked because the team member is consistently present in services. However, I can speak from personal experience that supporting a worship service is not the same as participating in one. Turning the action team into a small group that meets one evening every week will give the members an opportunity to bond and grow together spiritually. This type of training is just as vital to the overall health of the team.

Finally, it is important to keep the vision in front of the action team at all times. When the team takes ownership of the media ministry vision, then every aspect of their work will be tempered with that understanding. This will give a greater purpose to what may seem like work for some. The small group is a great place to reinforce the media ministry vision.

When these concepts are put into practice, a media ministry action team can be up and running in no time. A finely tuned and well-conditioned team will propel a media ministry to continual success.

Chapter 4

Action!

The equipment is in place, the vision established, and the teams have been formed and are poised. Time for the curtain to be raised and the media ministry put into action! Introducing media to a church can be both simultaneously exciting and terrifying. This chapter will give some practical tips on how to side-step potential problems and make the transition as smooth as possible.

Take It Slow

Especially in long-established churches, it is important to integrate a new media ministry slowly. I remember the first service utilizing media at Calvary Baptist Church in Las Cruces, New Mexico, where I first served as media minister. Calvary was a very cutting-edge church circa 1996, complete with a full praise band, four services, and two pastors—each with his own dynamic brand of preaching. Initially I had been hired as publications director. My duties were expanded to include media when our church purchased a new projection system. I was so excited! I spent a solid month preparing for the first service. Finally the day came. The screen lowered, the projector fired up, and the colors flew! I had a different background for each song. I also had a unique font for each song and tried to match the font style and colors to the feel of the song. During the sermon there were animations galore. After the services that weekend I learned that I had put my church into serious shock! Everyone—not just the older congregation members—had been overwhelmed. I asked a friend of mine who was my age what he thought. "I don't know," he responded. "There was just something not right about it."

I learned the hard way that I had simply introduced too much too soon, even for our cutting-edge church.

Media should be gradually introduced to a church. The congregation should be given time to get used to the idea of having a screen in their auditorium. It can be a big adjustment for everyone. The staff needs to ease into implementing this new form of communication as well. All of the proverbial cards do not need to be shown at once. In time, the church members will become accustomed to, and even crave, more media in their services.

The Entertainment Factor

Part of people's initial unease with media has to do with the feeling that it is inappropriate—too entertaining or irreverent—for the church. This is a natural reaction for many churched people. We briefly brushed against this subject in **Chapter 1**. There are two main keys to understanding and dealing with the concern about worship becoming entertainment. The first is that every person has a "line" when it comes to media—a line between what feels worshipful or what feels like distraction or entertainment. When trying to use media effectively, there will always be a risk of crossing someone's line. This line is different for each person. The "fun" part of media is somewhat like sugar in tea: Some like a lot of sugar, while others don't like any. The perceived amount of entertainment value in a church service often simply comes down to a matter of taste. Even so, it is important to determine where the entertainment line (or sugar level) is for the church as a whole. While it is impossible to please everyone, there needs to be a strong sense of what the general tolerance level is. As you try to determine this, be aware the people who object the most will also be the most vocal. To get a realistic pulse, you will need to gather a great deal of feedback from all types of church members. This will help determine where that line is for the majority of the congregation. Some church leaders do not ask questions about new concepts because they are afraid to hear what people think. Or worse, they guess at what people are thinking. Perception is everything, so it is critical to find out what the perceptions are. Adjustments to the media ministry vision may be made after hearing the various opinions of the congregation. If the vision team perceives that the church is not ready for all it has planned, but also feels strongly about implementing the vision, then the team needs to make a conscious effort to work on gradually "moving the line" so that the vision may be carried out.

Second, finding the appropriate balance between worship and entertainment requires understanding the nature and purpose of the worship service. There is a time and a place for everything during the course of a service. To determine where the entertainment element of media fits in, we will examine two basic aspects of a service, giving and receiving. During worship, media should be used to *support* the service and enhance the worship experience. Worship is a "giving back" time, not a receiving time. Any media used during worship should not distract people from focusing on God. In my opinion, media should be used with caution during the time in the service dedicated to the giving of tithes and offerings. Because this time is an integral part of worship, it is not appropriate to flash the announcements on the screen. The receiving parts of a service, such as the sermon, announcements, and special music, are great times to exploit the power of visual communication. When the implementation of media is balanced in this way is when it will be most effective.

There are times when media may not be used at all. Although I am obviously a huge advocate of using media during a church service, sometimes technology just needs to be switched off. Because of the work, manpower, and money involved in developing a media ministry, some churches may believe media should always be used or they won't be getting the most for their efforts. It is important not to forget about other means of communication such as using props, lighting, and even silence (on which everything is built). I have heard it said that a screen should never go black; however, in my opinion the screen represents only one component in an array of communication tools. Blacking out a screen can redirect attention to another part of the auditorium. A church service is a live event, not a movie. If the screen is always filled, the eventual tendency may be to ignore it as it blends in with the rest of the church décor. The only situation when the screen should be on at all times occurs when using IMAG, or live video, in a large church. In this case, having continuous projection is necessary to help people see what is happening on stage.

The Three P's of Implementing Media

There are three key elements required for successfully using media in your church. The first is **P**lanning. Gone are the days of finishing a sermon on Saturday night or throwing together a worship service at the last minute. Using media takes forethought, planning, and work. A pastor once told me that he just could not change the method he used to prepare services. "It's just the way God made me," he said. "I finish my sermon Saturday night or Sunday morning." I suggested that he take extra time one week and prepare *two* sermons. That way he would be ahead by one week from then on. Another possibility would be to let someone else preach one week in order to get ahead. If a pastor or music minister is not willing to make extra efforts to give the action team time to prepare quality media, then that church will never experience the full potential that visual communication has to offer.[4] It is simply not possible to rise above mediocrity without adequate time to develop a quality presentation. Therefore, the church leadership needs to decide if they want to simply support "church as usual" with a glorified overhead projector, or if they want to be a church that utilizes media to its fullest potential. The latter choice will ultimately yield a bigger crop.

The second P is **Patience.** Ask any megachurch about what it takes to get to their level, and they will tell you that it was a long process for them. No church will transform into a Willow Creek or Fellowship Church overnight. Developing the skills and acquiring the proper equipment to achieve a quality media ministry take time. It should be expected that mistakes will be made and that not every production will be an award winner.

Finally, using media in ministry also takes **Practice.** As with anything, it takes training and experience to develop an effective media ministry. With each passing service the action team will continue to improve its skills, whether in graphics, video production, or even in something as simple as the timing of switching slides. Those involved in running media should spend time with the pastor to become familiar with his or her sermon. The person running the software for showing songs during worship should definitely attend rehearsals to practice along with the group (more on that in **Section 3**).

Know Your Limits

Most of us ignore the credits that zoom by at the end of a television show or movie. At the next opportunity, take a moment to look at how many people it takes to put together a half-hour program. Sometimes hundreds of people have a hand in the production of a single show, even poorly produced ones! Though some have said that churches bear the responsibility of keeping up with the status quo in terms of production quality, it is unrealistic to think that the majority of churches have the resources to meet the standards set by production studios with hundreds of employees. A media ministry team should always strive to do its best, but also understand its limitations. The work involved in creating electronic media may seem easy to those who do not comprehend the complexity of production. Knowing what the team is capable of will help avoid conflict and misunderstanding when the team plans various media projects. Once the team members know what they can achieve, they can always strive to reach beyond that level. This way, expectations will always be met and sometimes exceeded.

There may be some occasions when it is best to outsource the production work. For instance, if the church would like to air a television commercial but does not have the proper equipment to produce a quality commercial, they should hire a professional to do it for them. Any advertising efforts exposed to the general public should be top-notch. There is a flood of poorly produced Christian programming in the public marketplace. A high-quality commercial will set the church apart and achieve better results.

Strive for Excellence, Standing in Grace

The word *excellence* has become a staple in church lingo over the past ten years. We have come to believe that everything from church administration to worship services should be executed with excellence, insinuating "without flaw." Some may be surprised to learn that the concept of excellence came from a business paradigm called "Total Quality Management." *Excellence* as defined by the Total Quality Management model is not necessarily a Biblical principle. The Bible refers to the excellence of God and charges us to strive for moral excellence, but nowhere in Scripture does it command us to conduct a flawless service. (In fact, according to a ChurchMedia.net poll, the majority of media ministries make up to five mistakes relating to media in each service.) The idea that excellence is a necessary component for achieving a growing and effective ministry has put a great deal of pressure on church leaders and laypeople. This demand is dramatically compounded for someone in charge of a media ministry.

Personally, I called *excellence* the "E word" in my tenure at Calvary Baptist Church. The word was used extensively and permeated every aspect of church operation. As a beginner with limited resources with which to work, the idea that I could achieve the production excellence expected of me was almost laughable. Being in charge of the most visual aspect of a worship service places a tremendous demand on any media minister. The weight of this existing pressure and the expectation of excellence became too much for me bear. I became very self-conscious about my work and felt that I was never quite meeting the expectations of the staff. I began to doubt my abilities and started to think that I was inadequate for the job. When church employees begin to feel that they are failing the church staff, it is easy for them to start to believe that they are failing God as well. When I realized this was happening to me, I began to strongly resent the concept of excellence in the church. This was obviously not healthy, and did, in fact, affect my work. Because the demand for excellence was so high, it actually had the reverse effect in my situation.

For years I hung on to this "anti-excellence" attitude. Once I was explaining my stance on the topic to a friend, and he said, "Sounds like grace was not in the picture." I discovered he was right. Though I'm sure it was not intentional, the staff never balanced the concept of excellence with the grace that we all experience as Christians. This revelation caused me to completely reconsider the idea of excellence. Only when excellence is tempered with grace will the pressure that striving for excellence naturally creates be relieved.

When assigning a task to media ministry team members, it is perfectly acceptable to ask that they do their best and even use the "E word." After all, God definitely deserves our excellence. I also believe that most people want to achieve excellence in everything that they do. However, when placing this challenge before someone, a church leader should always lace his or her statements with encouragement. Team members should feel that the church leader has confidence in their abilities. They should also be assured that there is forgiveness if they fail. Here are some examples of how to temper excellence with grace when speaking to someone:

> "I really want this video to look like the show we saw on TV last night, and I know you will do your best."

> "That wasn't exactly what I envisioned, but you did a good job. What would it take to do this...?"

> "Hey, the media team really didn't do so hot last week. There were several distractions that I'm sure we can avoid in the future. I know your team is capable of more. They did a great job a couple of weeks ago. Is there anything I can do to help?"

> "Great job last week! I really appreciate the dedication and hard work that you put in. Your ministry adds so much to our church."

Using this type of language will reinforce confidence in staff members and laypeople in a media ministry. Too much emphasis on excellence without enough encourage-ment will drive people away and out of ministry—perhaps even out of church life. A church that creates an atmos-phere of excellence balanced with grace will generate a healthy and powerful team of ministers. This team, in turn, will help foster spiritual growth within the church as it strives to achieve a higher standard of quality in every-thing that it does.

Always Have a Backup Plan

Disaster is inevitable when using technology in ministry. It is not a matter of *if* it will happen; it is just a matter of *when.* The day will come when the projector will not fire up or the computer will not boot up. On occasion, the video may not be cued to the right place (even though it was checked five times) or a song scheduled to be sung mysteriously disappears from the program. Knowing and expecting that something will eventually go wrong gives the media ministry team the opportunity to plan for such occasions.

A well-formulated backup plan will get the team through those rough times. Files should be backed up to another computer every week, perhaps on the secretary's computer. That old overhead projector should be ready for action if needed. The most useful talent for surviving a disastrous service is one's ability to "wing it." Church leadership and the media team need to be able to smooth over mistakes with charm and a determination to make the best of it. Above all, every person involved in conducting the worship service must keep his or her cool when disaster strikes. Showing distress or losing one's temper as a result of technical problems completely negates one's witness. Anyone seeing this type of behavior would (and should) question the spiritual maturity of that person. God can be worshiped with or without technology. With a good backup plan in place, church leaders can avoid any tendencies to become upset and continue with the service.

No Compromise

Finally, never compromise the Word of God for the sake of using media. Media ministry is still a new and growing field. Quality pre-made resources can be hard to find. Although up-and-coming companies are generating new material, the choices are still rather slim. When selecting media for use in church, always closely examine its theology. Make sure that what is being used falls in line with the beliefs of your church and does not conflict with Scripture.

It's About Communication

When applying the ideas in this book, always keep in mind that media ministry is primarily about effective communication. The tools of media should be used in concert with other traditional elements of worship with the goal of having a greater impact for the Kingdom of God. It can be easy to get caught up in the money and equipment needed and forget this basic principle. The concepts presented here will have more stability when built on this root idea.

Chapter 5

Copyrights

I always have a built-in alarm in my conscience when it comes to copyright issues, and could detect when it was wrong to copy something without actually knowing the law. Up until a few years ago, my convictions about copying material amounted to no more than just another opinion. But when I created my own graphics, the copyright issue became very personal to me when I released a collection of my work for the church market. There was a period of time when the sales from this collection were my sole income and support for my family. Any sharing or copying by churches would literally take food out of my children's mouths.

Copyright laws are often misunderstood or unknown by churches using media. They can be difficult to interpret. Below are twenty common questions that will help clear up some of these issues. I have purposely left out the "Fair Use" provision in the 1976 and 1998 Copyright Acts, which is a complicated subject and should be explored in detail by churches to see if they fall under this protection. In most cases, churches do not qualify for Fair Use. This act is often misinterpreted and may be abused by churches that do not want to take the time to make sure that they are following the law.

As a disclaimer, please be aware that laws can be subject to interpretation and sometimes change. These questions have been answered according to my understanding of copyright laws, and do not constitute legal advice. The number-one way that a church can make sure that they are not breaking any laws is to ask permission from the author or copyright holder when using their material. Several resource websites for finding out copyright information are listed in **Appendix G**.

The next time that you consider sharing a piece of material, whether it is a video, graphics, music, or otherwise, just remember that it does affect the creator of that work. A real person will lose money as a result. (If it helps, you can think of me!) However, I believe most church leaders and media ministries want to follow the law, so let's take a look at the top twenty copyright questions.

Top Twenty Copyright Questions

1. What type of license do I need to show songs in PowerPoint or worship software?

Christian Copyright Licensing International (CCLI) issues licenses to churches that display Christian song lyrics. A church must have this license and display the copyright information on at least one slide for each song. The copyright information and CCLI number for the church must be legible. Keep in mind that CCLI covers approximately 50 percent of popular Christian music. Not all music is covered.

2. What type of license do I need to show movie clips in a service?

For churches to show clips from popular movies, a motion picture license must be obtained. The Motion Picture Licensing Corporation is working with CCLI to provide a Church Video License through a new company called Christian Video Licensing International (CVLI). This license will cover the public display of movies from a large number of movie companies.

3. Can I digitize the movie clip I would like to show on Sunday so I can play it back from within my presentation software?

Unfortunately, no you can't. Although it would certainly make it more convenient, you are technically making a copy of the movie when it is digitized, and that is illegal if permission is not obtained. The clip needs to be played back from the original source (videotape or DVD). With a little practice, cueing and playing movies can become second nature.

4. Can I show a clip of something that I recorded from television?

Although it is legal for you to record the broadcast, you must obtain permission to show it in public. Television studios are very reluctant to give permission, so don't be surprised if your request is denied.

5. Can I use a clip from a movie in my video production?

No. Most movies stipulate that they cannot be transferred or altered in any way from the original. Taking out a portion of a movie to use in a video production alters the context of the movie and therefore constitutes a change. This also means you cannot edit out the bad language in a clip to use in church. Footage to be used in a video production must be royalty-free. There are many companies that offer royalty-free footage, including some very old movies.

6. I want to produce a video parody on a movie or TV show. Is that okay?

Parodies are covered under Fair Use and do not require permission. However, keep in mind that there are limitations. Material that could be considered slanderous or libelous is not protected.

7. Can I use company logos in my graphics or video productions?

Not usually. Almost every company with a logo will require permission to use their logos in any video, presentation, or printed material. You should always request permission.

8. I took my video camera and did some "man on the street" interviews. Do I need permission to use the footage?

Whether you interview someone on the street or as part of a specific project, it is prudent to have him or her sign a release statement, allowing you to use the recording. A sample release is in **Appendix I**. At the very least you should ask, "May I ask you a question?" when approaching people on the street.

9. We videotape our services. Is it okay to duplicate and sell them, give them away, or stream them from a website?

If your recording contains any copyrighted material, such as a recording of a soloist, then you must obtain permission from the owner of the material. In the case of special music, the producer of the soundtrack and the songwriter each have separate copyrights. The songs sung during worship are covered about 50 percent of the time under the CCLI license. There are some restrictions, however. Check with CCLI for details.

10. Can I save something off the Internet and use it in a presentation?

Not usually. The Internet is not fair game for free graphics. Most websites have a copyright notice that covers the entire site, which includes the protection of its images, text, design, and source coding. If a graphic is free for use, the website owners will usually make it a well-known fact. You should assume that copyright law protects all graphics on a site. When in doubt, ask for permission.

11. Can I scan a picture out of a magazine and use it in my presentations?

The content of magazines is covered by copyrights in the same manner that a website is. You need permission.

12. Can I take a picture of any object and use it in a graphics project or presentation?

You cannot, of course, take a picture of a picture, including famous paintings. You can take pictures of objects that you own or are on public property and use them in your graphics projects.

13. I have a great library of graphics. Can I share my graphics collections with other churches?

In most cases, the answer is no, not even one image. When a collection is purchased, each image is subject to the licensing agreement of the collection. Most of these license agreements state that you may not transfer images to anyone else. Read the licensing agreement that comes with your graphics for details. If there is not a license agreement, you should contact the company and ask about it.

14. I created some graphics of my own. Can I share or sell them?

That depends. If you created the graphics completely from scratch (that is, took the pictures yourself or generated some graphics electronically), then the answer is yes. You may sell or give away graphics that are 100 percent original at your discretion. However, any images that include photos of people or objects on private property may be a violation of copyright law. It is best to get permission in these cases.

When you use images from other commercial graphics collections, make sure to check the license agreement to find out what is and is not allowed. Many royalty-free photo collections, for example, grant you a license to modify a graphic, but do not allow you to distribute the files electronically. Some even stipulate that you acknowledge their copyright license to material used in your graphics. Selling a collection of graphics created from source material that is copyrighted (this would include clip art and royalty-free graphics) is definitely prohibited because you would, in turn, be in competition with the company. If you want to sell your graphics, you should create them entirely from scratch.

15. I would like to put copies of all of our media software on several computers for my media team members. Is that legal?

This is legal only if you have obtained what is called a "site license." Buying a single copy of a program does not include a site license. However, you should consult the software license agreement for details about exactly what is allowed. For example, many of the worship software companies allow you to load copies onto multiple computers as long as you are using the software on only one projector.

16. Can I make backup copies of my software?

In some cases the software license does allow you to do this. However, you should check the license agreement to make sure.

17. My presentation has copy-protected material in it. Can I share it?

If the copy-protected material in the presentation can be extracted or altered in any way, you will need permission. If the presentation can only be seen with a viewer program and cannot be edited, then you do not need permission.

18. What if I ask for permission to use something and never get an answer?

Assume that you do not have permission.

19. I've created some of my own graphics or videos. How do I protect them?

As soon as you create an original work, copyright law protects it. You do not have to put a copyright symbol on your work, but you may do so at any time. For further protection and to fix the exact date of creation, you should register your work with the U.S. copyright office.

20. We are just a small church without much money. God doesn't mind if we bend the rules a little, right?

I think you know the answer to that one! CCLI and CVLI use a sliding scale according to church size for their fees. How much is it worth to know that you are complying with the laws of the land?

Section 2:
Graphics Workshop

Chapter 6

Graphics First

Every visual aspect of a media ministry has one common element: graphics. Graphics are the building blocks for PowerPoint presentations, video productions, websites, printed material, and more. When a media ministry team learns to master the art of graphic design, everything the team creates will look more professional. The overall quality of media can dramatically increase its impact in a church. In this section, we will explore some basic technical principles that are important for building graphics. I'll leave most of the creative process to you and your team. After reading this section, try out the graphics exercises included on the DVD.

I have found that most people in charge of media spend more time developing the presentation than creating quality graphics. Many also rely solely on PowerPoint for creating, editing, and delivering graphics for their presentations. However, PowerPoint's graphic capabilities are limited. PowerPoint should primarily be used as a vehicle to display high-quality graphics that are developed in another program. By using the techniques described in **Chapters 6** and **7**, you will learn how to spend more time on graphics and less time in PowerPoint, which will result in better presentations.

There are three reasons for spending more time on graphics. The first reason is that, "Clip art is easy, but it's also kind of cheesy." Most professional publications and presentations do not include clip art. Although it is easy to type in a keyword and insert a cute cartoon into a presentation, most clip art lacks the professional look that people are accustomed to seeing. Though clip art can be a useful tool when used in moderation, businesspeople and media ministers alike are guilty of overusing clip art in their presentations. Using photos and other graphic design elements will take presentations to a higher level.

Second, "Word Art is old news." Microsoft Office Word Art provides a simple and fast way to spice up the text in a presentation, but it has been so overused that it is readily apparent where it came from. Using a professional graphics program to generate text for PowerPoint will give presentations a unique look. People who are familiar with PowerPoint will wonder how you did it! To PowerPoint's credit, however, the Word Art feature in the XP/2002 version is more robust and has a cleaner look.

Finally, "It's not hard to look like a pro." Several years ago, my own work was amateurish and lacked professional flair, but with practice I learned to create great-looking graphics for my presentations and website. Graphic design can be learned. If I can do it, anyone can!

Create Professional Graphics With 3 Techniques

Adding three basic elements to your graphics will help give them a professional look. The first is *transparency*. When several pictures are inserted on one PowerPoint slide, their shape will almost always be rectangular. The result will be a slide simply filled with box shapes overlapping one another. For instance, a picture of a person usually has an unwanted background. There is no easy way to remove that background and make it transparent using PowerPoint alone. PowerPoint does have a transparency tool, but using it will not only change your image to a lower resolution GIF format (explained below) but will also make only one color transparent. Even if there is a solid color that can be made transparent, this tool usually leaves a jagged edge around the image. By using an image-editing program you can make selected parts of an image transparent before bringing it into PowerPoint, yielding better results. Images created with transparent attributes will blend into the slide and look less blocky. Images that are semi-transparent will show objects placed behind them for a unique look.

The second professional technique is the addition of a *drop shadow*. Shadows are very important in graphic design. Shadows give depth to an image and can help elements stand out from the background. They also add a level of realism that cannot be achieved by any other method. PowerPoint does have a very limited shadow function for text, but the shadow it creates cannot be blurred or distorted in any way. If the shadow is moved too far away from the text, then the text becomes unreadable. Again, using an external image-editing program to generate images and text with shadows (also with transparency) will give PowerPoint presentations more depth.

The final pro element for graphics is actually a group of special effects. These "layer effects"—which include effects such as beveling, outlining, and glowing—are described in more detail in the DVD exercises. These advanced effects allow you to add dramatic and unique properties to a graphic layout. All of these effects will be maintained with their transparencies when they are brought into PowerPoint.

When I show a presentation, I want to make people wonder, "Is he using PowerPoint? I didn't know it could do that!" Applying these techniques will ensure that people will more likely pay attention to the presentation precisely because it will not look like an average PowerPoint slideshow. Eyes will be drawn to the screen to see what comes next when these pro graphic elements are used.

Time Savers

Although I highly recommend that you spend as much time as possible to prepare the media for a service, I realize that most church workers are usually in a time crunch every week. Many people not only do not get the material for the service very far in advance, but they also may be able to devote only several hours to creating their presentations.[5] With this in mind, I'd like to suggest three ways to save time and still create quality media.

Build a graphics library. There is a plethora of high quality graphic resources available on the market. Having a comprehensive library of graphics on hand can save hours of searching for just the right image. It is also much faster to use a pre-designed, professional graphic rather than trying to create one yourself from scratch. **Appendix J** includes a list of recommended resources that offer material designed for both general use and also specifically for church use. Also listed are some popular websites that provide downloadable graphics. When searching for graphics on the Internet, use terms like "stock photos" or "stock images" in your search to bring up high quality sites that offer photographs. Once you've built a library of graphics, you should catalog them using some type of image cataloging program for quick retrieval.

Learn keyboard shortcuts. Believe it or not, I'm old enough to remember when the mouse was invented. I started out using an old IBM 8088 computer running DOS and two floppy drives. At that time, the main program I used was a MIDI sequencing program called Cakewalk (remember, I used to want to be a Christian rock star). I had learned all of the keyboard shortcuts for getting around the program. When I saw a friend using Cakewalk with this weird little gadget with a ball and two buttons to get around the program, he seemed to be moving in slow motion! I could literally accomplish two or three times as many tasks using keyboard shortcuts. Since its introduction, we have a become mouse-dependent society. However, almost all modern programs still incorporate keyboard shortcuts. I have compiled the more useful shortcuts for the programs covered on the DVD in **Appendix K**. Learning and using keyboard shortcuts can literally save hours of preparation time.

Take your own pictures. Even with a vast library of images at your fingertips, you may still find it faster to take your own pictures in some cases. For instance, if the pastor is using a stoplight as a metaphor in a sermon, it will probably be quicker to step outside and take a snapshot than to search the Internet or browse through countless CDs. You may also have difficulty finding an appropriate royalty-free image at the right resolution for a reasonable price. Taking your own pictures with a digital camera can be a fun and rewarding alternative.

Digital Cameras

Digital cameras continue to improve in quality and have become very affordable in recent years. Every media ministry should have a digital camera on hand. Digital images provide perfect source material for creating custom graphics for projection. Here are some specifications to consider when choosing a digital camera:

Megapixels. The number of megapixels in a digital camera determines the *resolution* at which the images can be captured. The higher the megapixel count, the higher the possible resolution. The number of megapixels you will need depends on how the images you take will be used. In most media ministry situations a camera with at least 2 megapixels is adequate for projection use. If the images are to be used for printing purposes, then a camera with a higher megapixel count should be considered.

Resolution. Digital cameras originally specified resolution rather than megapixels. Some cameras still carry this specification and are usually capable of images that are 320 x 240 or 640 x 480 pixels. Cameras that do not carry a megapixel rating are usually not adequate for media ministry use and should be avoided. (Resolution is explained in more detail on page 85, "Understanding Resolutions.")

Storage Medium. The next consideration is the type of storage medium that the digital camera uses. There are several popular types of "digital film." Although the type of storage medium will not affect the quality of the images taken with a digital camera, each different type of storage has its own advantages and disadvantages. In the end, it comes down to personal preference. The number of images that can be stored on any of these formats depends on both the capacity of the medium and the resolution of the pictures. Sony cameras incorporate the *Sony Memory Stick®*, which is about the size of a piece of stick gum and comes in capacities of up to 128 MB. *CompactFlash®* cards are larger than Memory Sticks but have a capacity of up to a whopping 1GB. The *SD™ Memory Card* from Panasonic is a small, thin medium similar to Sony's memory stick with up to a 256 MB capacity. (A 1 GB card was in development at the time of this printing.) Finally, the *Smart Media™* format comes in capacities of up to 128 MB.

File Transfer Method. Once the pictures have been taken, they need to be transferred to a computer for editing and displaying. So another important consideration when choosing a camera is how the image files can be transferred. At the very least, most cameras include a cable that attaches to the USB or serial port of a computer for transfer. Or simply removing the storage medium from the camera and inserting it into the computer also provides a convenient way to transfer images. Most notebook computers are equipped with a CardBus (PCMCIA) slot. CardBus adapters are available for most of the aforementioned memory types, making file transfer quick and easy. Some notebook computers feature multiple slots for various forms of media. External memory card readers that connect to a USB port are also available for desktop (as well as notebook) computers. Some read only one type of media while others include multiple slots. Quick transfer is important to a media ministry. One reason is simply to save time. Another would be the ability to take pictures before a service or during fellowship and transfer them for immediate display during a service.

Lens. The lens is arguably the most important part of a digital camera. A 3-megapixel camera equipped only with a small lens will simply produce high-resolution, substandard images. When choosing a camera, look for a larger, glass lens. Some higher-end cameras feature "name brand" lenses. Expect to pay more for a quality lens, but the difference is well worth the extra expense.

Zoom. There are two types of zooming on digital cameras: optical zoom and digital zoom. The optical zoom is the real zooming capability of the camera, while any zooming beyond that is magnified digitally. For instance, if the camera has an optical zoom of 3X and a digital zoom of 20X, anything beyond the 3X point would be digitally magnified. Using the digital zoom usually creates undesirable artifacts in an image. The image will not be crisp and will look distorted. These effects are usually not noticeable on the small camera LCD screen. It would be disappointing to discover that after taking a bunch of pictures they were unusable. For this reason, I highly recommend turning off the digital zoom on any camera. So make sure you find out the optical zoom capabilities of a camera, particularly since the digital zoom specification is often what is most clearly labeled on the camera.

Understanding Resolutions

After you have acquired the proper camera, you will need to set it to capture images at an appropriate resolution. The numbers relating to resolution represent the number of pixels wide by the number of pixels high. More pixels will yield a more detailed picture. To understand resolutions, consider your own experience with the evolution of computer monitors.

640 x 480 (VGA). When you owned a 14-inch computer monitor, the resolution of your computer graphics card was set to 640 x 480 to accommodate the resolution capabilities of your monitor. This is also the still the resolution of standard video and television.

800 x 600 (SVGA). When you ran out and bought a 15-inch monitor, hopefully you changed the resolution settings on your graphics card to 800 x 600. Everything on your screen seemed to shrink, but you just gained more desktop space.

1024 x 768 (XGA). Then when 17-inch monitors became affordable you wanted the extra two inches. You may have tried to change the graphics card settings to 1024 x 768 only to discover that your graphics card could not output resolution that high. So, you either bought a new card or a new computer so that you could take advantage of the bigger monitor. Again, the icons on your screen seemed smaller, but you soon became used to the new look and the extra space.

1152 x 864 (SXGA). Finally, you settled on a 19-inch monitor and changed your graphics settings once again, this time to 1152 x 864. Satisfaction at last!

Coming Soon: 1366 x 768 (Wide XGA). One day the widescreen format will become standard in our society. Read the "Go Wide" article in **Appendix A** for more details.

Because projectors are high-resolution devices, it is important to understand what is meant by these resolution designations. The ability of a projector to display images in higher resolutions means that projectors are more like computer monitors than televisions. This is why computer images look much brighter and more colorful when projected than a video, which often looks dingy and colorless. Projectors, like computer monitors, have a native resolution at which they will best display computer graphics. Many projectors on the market today have a native resolution of SVGA (800 x 600) or XGA (1024 x 768). After learning the native resolution of a projector, set the graphics card output to match the projector's resolution. To change the resolution setting in Windows, right-click on the desktop, select Properties, and then click the Settings tab. The output resolution can be adjusted here. These same settings may be adjusted on a Macintosh by choosing **Control Panels > Monitors** and selecting the matching resolution from the list.

Understanding resolution is also important as it pertains to taking digital photos and creating images for projection. The resolution setting on a digital camera should match or exceed the native resolution of the projector being used. For instance, if the church owns a XGA projector, the camera's resolution should be set to 1024 x 768 or higher. If you are designing a graphic layout from scratch, you will also need to set the blank canvas or document to 1024 x 768. The resolution of an image can always be lowered, but it cannot be increased without noticeable image distortion. In other words, bigger is better.

One last setting to understand in relation to resolution is DPI, or dots per square inch. Without going into much detail, the DPI for images destined for the projection screen should be set at 72 or 96, while images for print should be set at 300 DPI. To fully understand how resolution and DPI are applied in a practical media ministry situation, be sure to go through the DVD graphics exercises.

Graphic Formats

Images may be saved in a variety of file formats. The extension or ending of a file name indicates its format. The file name is followed by its extension, which is separated by a period (**e.g. filename.extension, pastor.jpg**). It is important to understand graphic formats because each format has its own application. When you create graphics, you can save the same image in a variety of formats. For instance, a graphic designed for a sermon theme could be saved in one format for PowerPoint, another for printing, and yet another for the church website.

Your computer may be set to hide file extensions from view. To show these extensions, start Windows Explorer by holding down the **Windows** button on your keyboard and pressing **E**. Click the **Tools** menu and then **Folder Options**. Now click the **View** tab and uncheck the box next to "Hide extensions for known file types." Click **OK**. All file extensions will now be shown.

Formats for Web Use: Most of images that appear on websites are GIF (pronounced like *gift* without the t) and JPG (pronounced *J-peg*) file formats. The GIF format was designed specifically for web use and will download very quickly. GIFs will maintain transparency, even in Power-Point, though the number of colors and levels of transparency are limited. JPGs, however, may be saved at a variety of quality levels, making it the most versatile and most common format. When used for the Internet, JPGs are usually saved with more compression, making the file sizes smaller for quicker downloads.

Formats for Printing: When saving a file for print use, the best format to use is *TIF* (sometimes *TIFF*). A high resolution TIFF image saved at 300 DPI will look great when printed. Most commercial printers prefer TIFFs though JPGs saved at a higher quality level also work well for printing in many cases.

Formats for Video Use: Still images to be used for video production should be saved as a medium- to high-quality JPG or TGA (pronounced *targa*) file format.

Formats for Presentations: JPG images also work well for presentation use. A more useful file format for presentations is the PNG (pronounced *ping*).

The Best-Kept Secret

When used in combination with Adobe® Photoshop® or Photoshop® Elements (described below), the PNG file format is PowerPoint's best-kept secret. PNG files saved in Photoshop will maintain all transparency attributes of an image when used in PowerPoint. The best way to understand the power of the PNG format is to see it in action. In your *Graphics Workshop* folder, open the *png Examples* folder, and then the file called *png.ppt* (PowerPoint 2000 or XP is recommended for best results). Start the presentation and click your mouse to bring in each object. Notice the detailed transparency in each picture. Even small areas such as the spokes in the wheels of the old farm equipment are transparent. The edges around the rose are very clean. The glow around the text maintains a transparency that actually fades into the background. The shadow of the cowboy is overlaid on top of the entire image and is semi-transparent. All of these images are PNG files created in Photoshop. Stop the PowerPoint presentation and move the images around on the screen. Try resizing them as well. Notice that they maintain transparency no matter where you place them, and that they do not pixilate or distort when resized.

Photoshop and Photoshop Elements

Adobe Photoshop has become the standard program in image editing. For years I resisted using Photoshop because of the price and the learning curve. Both of these problems have recently been alleviated. Photoshop versions 6.0 and 7.0 are much more intuitive and include more standard user interface components. The full version of Photoshop 7 currently retails for approximately $600, which may make it cost-prohibitive for many churches. The solution is Photoshop Elements (2.0), which is a scaled-down version of Photoshop that retails for about $100 (not including available rebates). Photoshop Elements has been hailed as a breakthrough in consumer-level image editing. The look and feel of Elements is identical to Photoshop in many ways and provides a no-compromise alternative. Photoshop and Photoshop Elements files are interchangeable; someone could create a project in Photoshop and someone else could work on the same file in Elements. The native Photoshop file format is PSD, which keeps all of the layers of the image separated and allows for further editing. When saving images for different applications, you should start with the original PSD file.

To maintain transparency with PNG files in PowerPoint, the images must be saved using Photoshop or Elements. To date, I have not found another image editing program that maintains this transparency. Although there may be others that will keep the transparent attributes of a PNG file, it is still a good idea to learn and use Photoshop for image editing. It will continue to develop into a more powerful program and is the standard application used by graphics professionals.

Three Key Design Concepts to Remember

Before diving into the exercises on the DVD, there are three key concepts to remember when designing graphics. Share your *original* graphics with other churches. First, be sure to read over the copyright guidelines in **Chapter 5** to understand what the word "original" means. Once you are sure that you legally can do this, you should network with other churches that use media and share your work with them. It is a shame that hours of work may be put into a project only to be shown once and then sit dormant on a hard drive forever. Sharing original work with other churches will save them time and give them an opportunity to experience your unique style and giftedness. It is also a great way to fellowship with other media ministries and to learn from each other.

See each project as a work of art. Many times the graphic design process can seem like a chore. It can be tedious and time consuming. To create quality material, it is important to put on an "artist's hat" and see things from a more creative point of view. When graphic design is seen as a creative process it becomes less like work and more like art.

"Projects are never finished, just abandoned." No one knows for sure who said this first, but filmmakers such as Spielberg have subscribed to this idea that no project ever seems to reach perfection. When working on a graphics design project, keep in mind that you will probably never get it to look exactly the way you want. You will need to learn to when it is time to abandon a project and move on.

DVD Exercises

Time to try out the exercises! You will probably want to install the trial version of Photoshop before viewing the workshop videos on the DVD.

Although all of the workshop exercises demonstrate PC versions of the software, you will find that most of the techniques shown are easily transferable to the Macintosh platform. (PowerPoint XP is the only real exception; Power-Point XP contains features not currently available in any Macintosh version of PowerPoint.)

Windows: To install the Photoshop trial, simply click the **Software Trials** button on the Main Menu. Then click the **Install Adobe Photoshop Trial** button to launch the installation program. Follow the onscreen prompts to complete the installation.

Macintosh: Click on the button at the bottom of the screen for **Install Trial Software** to open the **Adobe Software Trials** folder. Double-click the **Install Adobe Photoshop** file to launch the install program. Follow the onscreen prompts to complete the installation.

Be sure to wait until you are ready to go through the training before installing the trial software, because the trials are limited.

The exercise called "One For All" can be used for Easter or any time of the year. This project carries over into the Power-Point exercise and must be completed *before* going on to the PowerPoint training.

Photoshop Basics

Below are some of the technical concepts learned in the graphics workshop that you may need to refer to from time to time.

There are many tools to choose from in Photoshop. Located below is a layout of the main tools that are used in the exercises. The letters in the parentheses are the keyboard shortcut keys. Simply type the letter to select the tool to use. These shortcuts work for both Windows and Macintosh versions.

Tools Relevant To The DVD Exercises

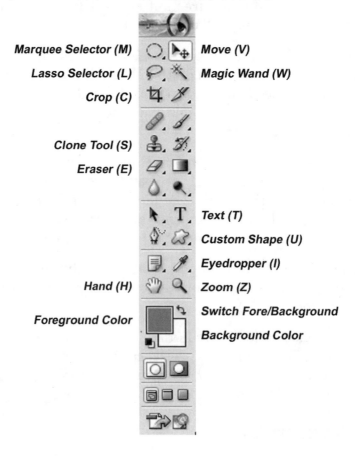

Marquee Selector (M)   Move (V)

Lasso Selector (L)   Magic Wand (W)

Crop (C)

Clone Tool (S)

Eraser (E)

    Text (T)

    Custom Shape (U)

    Eyedropper (I)

Hand (H)   Zoom (Z)

Foreground Color   Switch Fore/Background

    Background Color

Layers

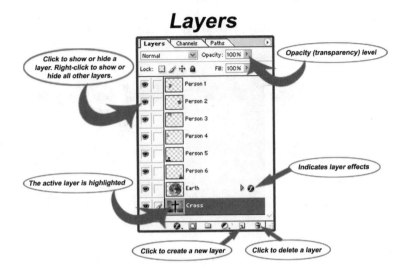

Click to show or hide a layer. Right-click to show or hide all other layers.

Opacity (transparency) level

The active layer is highlighted

Indicates layer effects

Click to create a new layer

Click to delete a layer

Unlike most Microsoft programs, layering objects is quick and easy in Photoshop. Rather than using a "move to front" or "send down one layer" type of system, Photoshop shows all layers in a hierarchy. Layers are simply dragged up and down the list to move from front to back. Note the other functions in the layers box.

Saving individual layers as PNG files:

1. Right-click the **View**  icon beside the layer to save and choose "Show/Hide all other layers."

2. Under the **Image** menu click **Trim**. Click **OK**.

3. Press **Shift+Ctrl+S** on your keyboard for **Save As**.

4. Choose **PNG** under **Format**, name the file, and click **Save**.

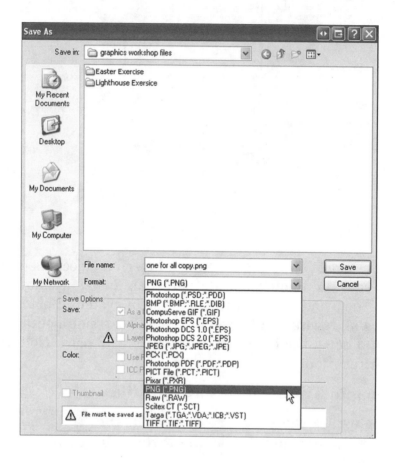

Section 3:
PowerPoint and Worship
Software Workshop

Chapter 7

Creating Dynamic Presentations

PowerPoint XP—It's a Whole New Program

In the **Graphics Workshop** exercise on the DVD, we created a graphic theme with a collage of pictures. We saved the individual pictures as PNG files; maintaining their transparency, drop shadows, and effects such as bevels and glows. We learned that PowerPoint should be used as a vehicle to display rather than create our high-quality images. In this section we will cover some presentation basics and also learn about special software designed specifically for use during worship. After reading through this section, try out the exercises on the DVD, which utilize the graphics designed in the graphics workshop. Be sure to also try some of the demo worship presentation software included on the DVD.

As I have mentioned, this book and the workshop exercises are presented from a PC perspective. For the most part, the principles and techniques presented are relevant for all media ministry teams, no matter which computer platform they use. However, many of the new features included in PowerPoint XP are simply not currently available in any of the Macintosh versions of PowerPoint.

PowerPoint Grows Up

According to an informal poll I took, 90 to 95 percent of all churches using media use Microsoft PowerPoint as their main display software.[6] Since PowerPoint comes as part of the Microsoft Office package, many churches already own it. As a result, churches all over the world have been using PowerPoint in innovative ways for years, bending this business application to meet their needs.

At my first post as media minister in 1996, I used a presentation software application called Astound® Presentation. I compared it to the PowerPoint of its day and found Astound to be superior in many ways. It had advanced animation control and interactive programmability. For a number of reasons I eventually switched my loyalties to PowerPoint, but longed for the advanced features I had utilized in Astound. With each passing upgrade to PowerPoint I looked for these features to be included. Finally, with the XP (also known as 2002) version of PowerPoint, my dreams came true.

PowerPoint XP represents a huge leap from previous versions. So much so that it is almost like a new program. It features an advanced visual timeline for complete control of animating objects on a slide. Objects can enter simultaneously and even exit before the end of the slide. Dozens of new, professional transitions and effects have been added. The entry and exit path of objects may now be literally drawn, giving complete control over the position of an object and its path animation. There is also a "presenter's view" included for dual monitor setups (explained later). All of these new features are demonstrated in detail in the DVD exercises.

Every church doing media in ministry should strongly consider PowerPoint XP for announcements, sermons, and special presentations. Churches with an older version of PowerPoint can upgrade to the XP version for around $100.[7] The upgrade is available at most office and computer stores. PowerPoint can be upgraded independently of other Office programs, so an Office upgrade is not necessary. If your church does not already own a version of PowerPoint, Microsoft has started a charitable pricing program. Contact your denomination or conference head office and inquire about potential group licensing that they may have in place. The charitable price on Microsoft Office XP is unbelievably low, making it affordable for any size church.

The animations in PowerPoint need a certain amount of computing and graphics power to work properly. Refer to **Chapter 2** for suggestions on computer specifications for a media ministry computer. Having a robust graphics card and plenty of system RAM are the two most important system requirements for using PowerPoint XP. If the computer is lacking in these areas, elements on a slide may not transition quickly or smoothly.

The PowerTeam

In **Chapter 3** we learned about the importance of building a strong media ministry action team. For churches that extensively use PowerPoint, an action team of no less than three people should be employed. Because there are three distinct elements that make up effective PowerPoint presentations, you will want to look for team members who excel in each of these areas.

The CompuGeek. Many times, all of the tasks of using Power-Point in church are assigned to the resident computer nerd. CompuGeeks play an essential role in a "PowerTeam" because they know all of the nuances of the program. They can get inside of PowerPoint and make it do things it wasn't designed to do. However, many CompuGeeks lack an eye for graphics and colors.

The Artist. That's where the artist comes into the picture (bad pun, I know). Most churches have at least one person with a knack for color coordination and gifted with a creative flair. With the CompuGeek at their side, the artist will make presentations look fantastic while getting the most out of PowerPoint.

The Musician. The third member of the PowerTeam should be a musician or vocalist. Ideally, the musician will actually run the presentation (be it PowerPoint or another application) during the song portion of a service. People who are familiar with the music are the best equipped to run the presentation because they know the sequencing of song and have a better sense of timing and rhythm. One effective way of filling this role would be to rotate a member of the worship team into this position once a month. This member of the PowerTeam does not have to be technical or artistic; he or she only needs to know the music well and have at least two fingers—one finger to press the key to advance the slides and another finger as a backup in case the first finger malfunctions. One caution, however: musically inclined people love to worship. You'll want to make sure that they have the ability to focus on doing their job. For example, I was at a rather large conference once and everyone noticed that the slide was not changing during a song. We all turned and gave the computer operator "the look" (you know, "the look" that you give sound and media people who are not doing a good job), but she didn't notice because she was praising God at full steam with her eyes closed and hands in the air.

Presentation Tips for Songs

Timing Is Paramount

Another extremely important responsibility of the person running the computer during worship is attending rehearsals. The computer operator is a vital member of the worship team and handles the most visual aspect of a worship service. Unrehearsed computer operators can cause major distractions in the worship service. The computer may be seen as an instrument that they must practice and then play during worship. As with any musical instrument, timing is paramount. In the case of the "computer instrument," the timing relates to when slides are advanced during a song.[8] Everyone has a different opinion: "You advance right on the beat." "No, you advance right on the last word of the slide." "No, it's the first word of the next slide." "No, it's three words back from the last word on the slide." And so on. There is simply no one right answer since the right time to advance the slide depends on several factors.

Here are a few tips for determining what works best for each situation:

- The rhythm of the song plays a big part in advancing the slides.

- Try to advance at a time that "feels" right and gives the congregation enough time to find their place. Only a good musician has this sense of timing.

- If there is a musical pause between slides, do not advance too quickly. This will make the song feel rushed.

- If there is no musical pause between slides, be sure to advance a bit early to ensure that no one misses any part of the lyrics.

- If there is a long musical interlude before the singing begins or between slides, either wait to advance or insert a blank (not black) slide during the musical part of the song. If the next verse shows during this time, the congregation will be concentrating on when to sing rather than appreciating the music. Another suggestion would be to display a slide with a Bible passage that pertains to the song or the theme for the day during the interlude.

Keep It Simple

Choosing which colors and fonts to use for song slides is another area of heated debate. Recall the story in **Chapter 4** where I described how I overwhelmed the congregation at my first media service. Obviously, I once held the opinion that you could enhance a song by dressing up the lyrics on the screen. After a couple of years of experimentation I decided that "simple is better" when it comes to displaying songs. The lyrics need to be read quickly and easily. The font should be a sans serif typeface like *Arial* or *Tahoma*. Serifs are the little "tags," or short decorative lines at the start or finish of a stroke on a letter, in serif typefaces like *Times New Roman*. Sans serif fonts make reading words on a big screen easier.

If the projector being used in the church is not as bright as it should be (as many church projectors aren't), you will want to use a contrasting color combination—one color should be dark and the other light—so that the text can be easily seen. A medium-blue background with white or yellow letters works especially well. This color combination will make the text easier to see. However, if the projector is bright enough, I suggest an "in between" solution. Try to use a background image that relates to the theme for the service. If the background is too busy, place a semi-transparent box on top of the image so that the text will stand out. Transparent boxes are a new feature of PowerPoint XP and are easily added and adjusted to any background (see PowerPoint exercises for instructions).

Using drop shadows and outlines on the text provides another method of making text stand out. This can be done in PowerPoint with Word Art, or in Photoshop by saving the text as a PNG file with transparency. The third and easiest option for adding outlines and drop shadows to text is to use a worship software program that incorporates this feature.

Fixing Mistakes

A time will come when every media minister will misspell something on a PowerPoint slide. Even with a spell-checker mistakes can be made. My biggest blunder was in the song "Higher Ground." To my horror, I had typed "where rears abound" instead of "where fears abound"! I quickly fixed the word for the next service. What was worse, however, is that I forgot to fix it in the original presentation and showed it again the following week. The moral of the story is to make sure that errors are fixed in the original song file when they are discovered. This is not an issue if worship software is used to display songs, because the songs are all in one database instead of several different files.

Worship Software: A Teaser

The best tip I can give concerning song presentations is to use worship software *instead* of PowerPoint. Worship software programs are designed specifically for church use and are more efficient than PowerPoint for displaying songs and Scriptures. More details on worship software are covered later and several reviews of these programs may be found in the appendices. These programs do not replace PowerPoint for other presentation applications, however, so let's cover some other presentation tips before going into more detail on this subject.

Presentation Tips for Announcements

Is Anyone Watching?

I have some sad news for churches that spend most of their time creating dazzling pre-service announcements—no one watches them. After the initial "wow" factor of onscreen announcements wears off, people go back to their usual routine of fellowshipping with other church members and ignore the images on the screen.[9] One problem is that many media ministers assume that a church is like a movie theater and everyone will be glued to the screen in anticipation of the service. We know that this is not the case, however. People at church generally like to catch up with other church members during the pre-service time.

There are several solutions to this problem. One unique solution is to not run onscreen announcements at all. This was the option that Hoffmantown Church in Albuquerque, New Mexico took. They noticed an interesting phenomenon when running announcements before a service. Not only were people ignoring the announcements, it would take at least two worship songs before the congregation settled down and entered a "worship mode." It seemed that the announcements were helping to create the wrong atmosphere for worship. They decided to try displaying only one slide as people came in. This slide contained a Bible verse and perhaps an image relevant to the theme for the service. They noticed an immediate improvement in the quality of worship. The congregation entered into worship more quickly because they were more focused on God and the service theme.

Add Audio

For those who would like to make the announcements work onscreen, adding audio to a PowerPoint slide is an easy way to attract attention to the screen. Every church has at least one person in the congregation with a good speaking voice, whether she or he knows it or not. Identify that person and have her or him come in to read a short script about an announcement. The narration can be recorded directly into a computer using a standard computer microphone and the Sound Recorder program included with Windows. The sound file (with a .wav extension) can be attached to a PowerPoint slide and will automatically play when the slide is shown. Using sound effects can also draw attention to the announcements. For instance, an advertisement for a youth car wash could include bubble noises. The amount of audio used will depend greatly on the type of church and the preference of what kind of atmosphere they would like to establish before a service. Many churches play praise music during this time, so any audio used in a presentation would have to complement the style of background music being played. A voice-over playing while someone is singing would, of course, be a disaster.

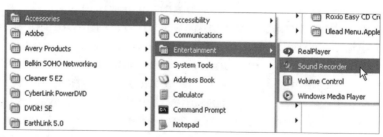

Figure 1: The Windows Sound Recorder program can be found in the *Entertainment* folder.

Print Is Also Media

Several years ago I went to a church in Texas to help them with their first media service. A new two-projector system had just been installed. Among other things, they handed me a stack of papers with announcements and Sunday school class schedules with room numbers. "What do you want me to do with this?" I asked. "Put it up on the screen," replied the music minister. "First of all," I responded, "I don't want to do it because it looks like a lot of work; but more importantly, don't you have this stuff printed in your bulletin?" "No," he said. "We told our board that we wouldn't have to print anything anymore and that's how we persuaded them to approve the video projectors." I explained that a person would have to be watching the screen at just the right moment to know where to go for Sunday school and everyone would need a photographic memory to recall all the announcements pertaining to the week's events. The music minister realized that materials would still have to be printed for the church.

This is an extreme case. Most churches realize that onscreen announcements will not replace printed material. However, many churches do not expend much effort on creating their printed material. The same principles learned in the graphics workshop can be applied to church bulletins. The good news is that any graphics generated in Photoshop for use in PowerPoint can also be used in print. Using the same graphics for presentations and in printed material is a great way to reinforce messages and provide a consistent look.

Advertising Rules

When creating and presenting announcements, be sure to follow standard advertising rules. If there is an important event that needs to be emphasized, incorporate this information several times throughout the presentation. Both radio and television advertising effectively employ the technique of repetition. Though you may think a commercial or its jingle is annoying, the message conveyed is difficult to ignore.

Also be sure to include all the important details of an event: what, when, where, and what to bring. Include the day (Tuesday, etc.) as well as a date. For times, always include AM or PM. Even if it is an announcement for a men's breakfast at 6:00, someone will invariably ask, "Is that 6:00 *in the morning*?"

Reinforce announcements with an appropriate image. Take care not to include irrelevant graphics such as cute cartoon characters that do not pertain to the announcement. Also avoid text-only announcements, because they are difficult to remember. An image that directly relates to the event will help people retain the information.

When Not to Show Announcements

I've seen some churches show announcements at audacious times during a service. One church showed announcements during the offertory. I suppose they thought this was a good way to make sure that people would see them, but I think it detracted from the spiritual nature of giving as a time of worship. Another church showed its announcements during special music behind the soloist. I'm not sure if she even knew that they were up on the screen, but as a former performer I know that it would make me furious to know that the Ladies Luncheon was being announced while I poured my heart out in song. Rather than displaying an announcements presentation at an inappropriate time to get people's attention, adding sound and high-quality graphics is a better way to encourage people to watch the announcements.

Video Announcements

Promoting events in the church need not be limited to using PowerPoint. Occasionally an announcement may be produced as a video instead. Video offers a wider array of tools for communication than PowerPoint. Consider producing a short "commercial" for special events. More information on video production can be found in **Section 4**.

Sermon Note Tips

Go Beyond Text

Putting sermon notes in PowerPoint in text format is quick and easy. Onscreen sermon notes that correspond with a printed fill-in-the-blank handout help increase attention as people refer to the screen to get the next "answer." Once this type of system is in place, the pastor and the media ministry team should strive to go beyond text-only and include pictures in sermon presentations. Just as with announcement slides, sermons with relevant graphics will help people retain and recall the sermon as they associate the points with the images.

As you come across various graphics, try to catalog the images according to how they might be used in a sermon. Building a database of where the images can be found and what themes they may relate to will help immensely when searching for appropriate graphics for a sermon.

Use Thematic Backgrounds

Rather than using one background for all PowerPoint slides—or worse, a different background for every slide—consider using a background theme-set. A theme-set is a group of graphics with the same basic design and colors, but with several variations on the master graphic.[10] Take a look at the example set called "Hotline" in the **Bonus Resources > Kick Starters** folder. Here are the types of backgrounds in this set:

Master Graphic. This graphic displays the main design on which the others will be modeled. "Hotline" shows a red phone with a cord fading into clouds. Notice that there is not much room for adding any other text.

Title Background. The title background differs from the main graphic by having just enough room for a sermon title to be added. In our sample set, the sermon has been called "Connecting With God." The title background introduces the sermon and the basic graphical design to go along with it.

Note Background. These graphics have plenty of room for sermon notes. Use one background for main points and a different one for sub-points. After a while, the congregation will subconsciously shift gears when a new point is introduced and the background changes slightly.

Scripture Background. This background contains a picture of the Bible in the corner and has enough space for displaying Scripture passages.

Song Background. This background has a tint over it so that text will be easier to read for songs. Using a song background during worship that corresponds to the theme of the service will set the stage for the sermon topic.

Welcome Background. This background may be shown during the greeting time. It will also help prepare people for the theme of the day.

Using the principles learned in the graphics workshop, anyone can create his or her own theme-sets. Thematic backgrounds give each Sunday a unique look and feel. At the same time, these backgrounds provide a consistency in the overall style for the service. This technique will enhance the overall quality of the message and help the congregation relate to the topic.

Planning and Practice

Let me reemphasize the importance of planning and practice. The pastor needs to give the media ministry team plenty of time to develop the graphics and presentation to support the sermon. I guarantee a noticeable improvement of the effectiveness of a message backed by a powerful metaphor and quality graphics.

Just as with the song presentation, practicing the timing for sermon notes is very important. The pastor should spend some time each week with the person who will be running the presentation so that they are familiar with the sermon. Many preachers may be concerned that the wrong slide is showing behind them, causing a sometimes-noticeable paranoia during the sermon. Devoting an hour or so to review with the PowerPoint operator will help alleviate this concern. Another option would be to have the pastor control the advancement of the presentation with a handheld remote mouse, as long as he or she is comfortable doing so.

PowerPoint Exercise

Now is a good time to try out the PowerPoint exercise on the DVD. To complete the exercise, you will first need to go through the graphics workshop if you have not already done so. The graphics created during that exercise will also be used in the PowerPoint training.

Following are some highlights of the exercises that you may need to refer to from time to time.

Working With the Advanced Timeline

To make the advanced timeline show up in the animation task pane, there are two necessary steps:

1. **Right-click** each of the animation lines and choose "Start with previous." Each animation line must be set this way for the timeline to show up for all of the images on the slide.

2. **Right-click** one of the animation lines and choose "Show advanced timeline."

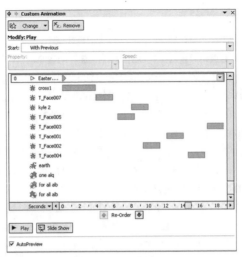

After performing these two steps, the timeline will be visible as shown above.

Place your mouse pointer in the middle of a transition and click/drag to move it forward or backward on the timeline.

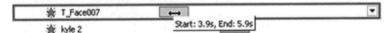

Move your mouse to the edge of a transition and click/drag to increase or decrease the timing.

To attach a sound file to a slide, choose **Insert** > **Movies and Sounds** > **Sound from File**. Answer "Yes" to the popup question. Move the speaker icon completely off the slide.

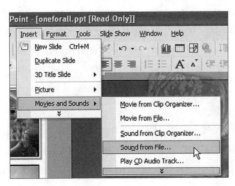

Worship Software

After going through the PowerPoint exercise, you will see that the XP version has become a powerful tool for delivering high-quality presentations. However, PowerPoint has always had one major weakness: its linear nature has made it difficult to prepare and operate presentations in a way that allows for the spontaneity that songs (and sometimes Scriptures) need. In order to deal with this shortcoming, churches have developed elaborate and innovative systems to make PowerPoint more worship-friendly. Even in churches that have mastered the use of PowerPoint for worship, there is still a possibility of error or delay in displaying songs that were not originally planned.

The XP version of PowerPoint has a new feature called the "presenter's view" that will show thumbnails of all of the slides and allow the operator to choose any slide at any time. This feature requires a dual-monitor setup, which is explained below. This is a step in the right direction, but it still does not provide a comprehensive solution for worship use.

Worship Software: A Brief History

When churches first began to use projectors to display song lyrics, PowerPoint's limitations during worship quickly became obvious. It was difficult to navigate and could take hours to prepare. Taking a vested interest in this problem, church-going computer programmers in all parts of the country decided to step up to the plate and design programs that would do a better job for worship purposes. As a result, there have been numerous presentation applications developed for churches. Some of these programs have matured into sophisticated applications that are the cornerstones for many media ministries.

Key Features

When I discovered this phenomenon in 1999, I took it upon myself to review as many of these programs as I could find and educate churches as to how these programs can be of benefit. After becoming familiar with the benefits and drawbacks of various programs, I have discovered several key features to look for when choosing worship software.

User friendliness. Naturally, the worship software needs to be very easy to use. Some programs are more intuitive than others, and they all have varying types of user interfaces and methods for displaying songs. There will inevitably come a Sunday morning when the person assigned to run the software will not show up for one reason or another. The most important question to ask is, "Can someone learn the basics of this software in ten minutes or less?"

Flexibility. Not all churches follow a set order of worship, and even those who do plan their music occasionally veer from the program. The worship software should be flexible enough for an operator to search for a song and quickly display it at a moment's notice. The quality of the search engines varies from program to program. This feature should be explored thoroughly to make sure that the worship software is flexible enough to meet the needs of your church.

Bible access. Another valuable feature of worship software is the ability to display Scripture from the program. Similar to the song-search feature, this feature allows an operator to look up a Bible verse or verses and immediately display them. Most worship software includes this feature. The number of Bible translations included with a program varies. Programs that include only one or two translations usually offer additional versions for a small fee.

Nursery alert system. Many churches incorporate some type of system to notify parents if they are needed in the nursery. Some churches use a number system with a display attached to a wall while other use pagers. Many worship software applications have a call system built right into the program. They will allow a number or short text message to be displayed in a corner of the screen. This number will remain visible until removed even as the song slides are changed. Some programs also have a messaging system that allows for longer lines of text to be displayed.

Video and audio support. As computer power continues to increase there will be many opportunities to incorporate video into worship software. Several of these programs already allow moving video backgrounds to be inserted behind text. In order to accomplish this composite of text and video, the computer being used needs to have adequate processing power, RAM, and graphics card power. Some worship software supports audio files as well. Sound effects, music files, and CD tracks may be accessed without the need to switch to another program.

PowerPoint integration. Some worship software will import a PowerPoint presentation and allow an operator to control the slideshow, usually with a thumbnail view of the show. There are advantages and disadvantages to this feature. The obvious benefit is that a PowerPoint presentation may be integrated with the song service without having to switch to PowerPoint. The downside to this feature is that most of the worship software uses the Microsoft® PowerPoint® Viewer, which is a 1997 version, to allow PowerPoint presentations to be viewed outside the program. Because this viewer uses technology from several generations back, it lacks many of the features of the current version of PowerPoint. Since Microsoft does not plan on releasing an updated viewer, my recommendation would be to have both PowerPoint and your choice of worship software open at the same time. Switching between the two programs is seamless and will allow you to take advantage of the full benefits of PowerPoint XP as well as the flexibility of the worship software.

Dual-screen operation. All of the worship software I have reviewed incorporates a dual-screen system to operate. Some will work with only one screen, but the programs really need dual outputs to get the most out of them.

Dual Screens

The majority of computer systems include a single monitor connection. Since Windows 98, however, the operating system software can actually support multiple video cards that allow more than one monitor to be connected to a computer. Software programmers creating worship applications have leveraged this feature to the advantage of churches using media. A computer equipped with two graphic outputs will be required to effectively use worship software. One output is connected to a standard computer monitor (a 17" or larger screen is recommended) while the second output is connected to the projector. The worship software will detect this configuration. The computer monitor will display a control screen that only the operator can see allowing him or her to choose songs, verses, choruses, Scriptures, and more without the congregation ever seeing the program. On the projector the congregation will see the full-screen results.

Graphics Cards for Desktop PCs

A desktop or tower computer to be used with dual-monitor worship software must be running Windows 98 or higher (XP is recommended) and be equipped with two graphics cards or a single card with two outputs. Current model computer motherboards come standard with an internal expansion slot designed specifically for graphics cards, called AGP (Accelerated Graphics Port). Other slots on the motherboard are called PCI slots. A computer using two graphics cards would incorporate an AGP graphics card and a PCI graphics card. A computer already equipped with an AGP card would need to have a PCI graphics card installed for the second output. Since the AGP card is superior in performance, it should be the card connected to the projector. The full-screen output will be doing more work than the control monitor. The PCI card should be connected to the control monitor.

Most computers will tend to boot up from the AGP card, and Windows will use it as the primary monitor. This is undesirable in a church setting since the AGP card is connected to the projector and will expose the boot-up screen to the congregation. Many motherboard BIOS settings can be adjusted to tell the computer to boot up using the PCI graphics card instead of the AGP. Ask a qualified computer expert to check the computer's BIOS for this option. In Windows XP, the primary monitor can be set to the PCI card in the **Display Settings** properties (see below). Making these two adjustments to the computer's software will ensure that the congregation never sees an unwanted computer screen.

Another solution would be to have an AGP card that has two monitor outputs. When using this option, it is important to find a card with plenty of graphics RAM and equal power on both outputs. Some dual-head cards lack 3-D acceleration or DVD decoding on the second output. Also, keep in mind that the graphics RAM will be split between the two outputs. Therefore, a card with 32 MB of RAM will yield 16 MB on each output. There are several models that are basically two graphics cards on one board. All features like 3-D acceleration and DVD playback are available on both sides. Since the graphics card is the heart of a media ministry computer, it is prudent to spend extra time finding the appropriate graphics card and perhaps budgeting extra money for a more powerful card.

Dual Screens for Laptop Computers

Churches using laptop computers with worship software have two options for using dual screens. The first and most desirable solution would be to purchase a laptop with adequate graphics RAM and built-in dual screen capability. In a laptop with dual screen capability, the screen attached to the laptop acts as the control screen while the monitor output, connected to the projector, displays the full screen graphics. Not all laptops are capable of this configuration, but most current model laptops do come with the dual screen feature. To determine if a laptop has this feature, check the **Display Settings**. If a picture of two monitors is showing (one will be grayed out), then the laptop includes the feature. Clicking on the grayed out monitor will activate the second display.

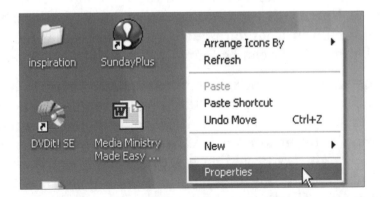

To check and adjust your display settings, **right-click** the desktop and choose **Properties**.

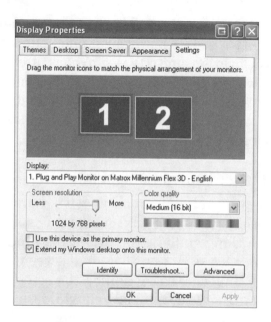

Click the **Settings** tab to configure your display settings. Notice that you can set either graphics card as the primary monitor.

As with desktop machines, the graphics resources on a laptop will also be split between the displays. You will therefore want to use a laptop with an ample amount of graphics RAM. At least 32MB of RAM is recommended. There are various brands of graphics chips available for laptops. The type of chip in a laptop is usually labeled somewhere on the laptop case or can be found in the display settings.

If the laptop cannot support dual displays, the second option would be to get a third-party graphics card that may be plugged into the CardBus slot of a laptop. Because currently the maximum RAM available on one of these cards is only 4 MB, adding a second card is not the most desirable option. However, if getting a new laptop is not feasible, then a CardBus graphics card will work. In this case, I recommend using the 4 MB card for the control screen and connecting it to an external computer monitor. Then you may use the laptop's graphics output for the projector.

Appendix L lists information on several worship software programs worth looking into. Try each program out in a worship setting to see which one works best for you. A comparison chart of programs and reviews may be found online at www.MediaMinistryMadeEasy.com.

Section 4:
Video Production Workshop

Chapter 8
Video Production

Convergence

At my seminars, eyes start to glaze over during the video production workshop. For many churches, just getting a media ministry to a basic level of competency with PowerPoint can be quite a challenge. The prospect of producing videos for church use can be overwhelming. In this section we will learn how easy and affordable video production can be. More importantly, however, let's first explore why a church should even make the effort.

To understand why one should learn video production, it is important to note the *convergence* of communication technologies in our society. Those who keep up with company mergers may have noticed that communications companies in the telephone, Internet, and entertainment industries seem to be interested in combining forces. These industries are looking closely at one another because they know that eventually there will be another type of convergence—the convergence of how communication data is transmitted. Put simply, there will come a day when all types of communication methods (e.g. audio, video, computer data) will be transmitted together through the same type of communication conduit. We have already seen the emergence of high-speed communication through DSL, cable, and satellite. These and other technologies will continue to improve to the point that all of our communication may be conducted through one device, which brings us to our third type of convergence—the convergence of communication devices. A good example of this type of convergence is the recent combination of PDAs (handheld computers) and wireless phones. With a single piece of equipment you can manage your schedule, check your email, and make phone calls. All of this is done through *one* device, via *one* type of communication conduit, through *one* company. Eventually your computer will be your telephone (or videophone) as well as your movie and music on-demand entertainment center. The possibilities are almost limitless.

If communication companies, transmission, and equipment will eventually converge, how will this revolution affect the church? The next time you go to a computer store, notice the selection of video editing software. I think you will be surprised at the selection. Software companies are meeting the demands of the general public for applications that make editing home videos easy and fun. The extent to which the public is using camcorders is constantly rising. The number of amateur videographers who captured the tragic events of September 11, 2001 on tape is evidence of this trend. Their footage was invaluable in helping the world see the reality of those events. When convergence matures and high-speed data transmission becomes a reality for most people, many will be streaming their video productions over the Internet in full-screen resolution. In other words, in addition to websites, many people will be running their own virtual television stations. Since we know that communicating through video will eventually become a major part of our society, the church has the opportunity to master this form of art *before* the real revolution is underway.

Not only is mastering video production important because of the upcoming changes in communication, it also simply provides a more dynamic way to use media. Despite the new animation power in PowerPoint XP, presentations seem to stand still compared to video productions. In this section as well as in the training exercises on the DVD, we will look at a number of examples and ideas for using video effectively in a church setting.

The Six Talents of Video Production

There are six areas of video production to master. As we have already learned in the section on teambuilding, a media ministry should not rely on only one person for a job requiring multiple talents. If necessary, six people should be recruited for a video production team, though one person may possess talents in several of these areas. Each of these positions is vital to producing quality videos that will stand out from average "point and shoot" videos. Substandard productions will only distract from the message, while videos that show creativity and attention to detail will communicate volumes of information in a way that no other medium can.

Drama director and coordinator. If there is any acting involved in a video production, the resident church drama person should be recruited to help. Having a drama director will be immensely helpful for any project that incorporates a script. A person trained in the dramatic arts can provide guidance on speech inflections and on improving voice clarity and projection. This person may also have a knack for coordinating the many elements—both people and locations—involved in a video project.

Video director. Good video directors are also usually big movie buffs. They do not go to movies simply for entertainment, but to rather critique the cinematography and other aspects of a film. They pay attention to production details like camera angles, framing, editing techniques, sound effects, and music. They may even closely examine character development, foreshadowing, and other methods of building a good movie plot. Having this person on the production team will help add creativity and professionalism to a church video production. He or she will want to create a video that not only has character in its message, but also in the delivery of that message.

Camera operator. Often, the video director will also be the camera operator. Whether or not this is the case, the camera operator needs to be trained about how to properly use a video camera. Camcorder marketing campaigns have led us to believe that anyone can pick up a camera and look like a pro. While that message may help sell camcorders, the truth is it takes practice and knowledge of basic video principles to properly use a video camera. A camera operator who does not have adequate talent and skill can ruin even the very best concepts.

Lighting director. Lighting is considered an art form in and of itself. You should recruit someone who is both experienced and zealous about lighting. We will discuss lighting in more detail below.

Makeup/wardrobe designer. Makeup and wardrobe are important aspects of any production, even for something as simple as an interview or testimonial. For instance, if the person being videotaped is bald, a little powder will help keep lights from reflecting and causing distraction. For clothing, bright reds should be avoided because they tend to "bleed" and streak. Striped shirts are also undesirable because they can create strange moiré patterns on a screen. These are just a couple of tips that a person qualified in these areas can help with. Many times a person involved in drama or theatre will be the best to put in this position.

Video editor. A good editor can take hours of raw footage and craft it into a coherent and artful whole. Like the video director, the editor usually loves movies and DVDs with behind-the-scenes footage. Good editors pay close attention to detail such as sound, background action, and even the rhythm of the transitions.

Video Production Prelude

Before going into the details of the equipment and techniques involved in video production, let's quickly cover a few basic ways that video may be used in a church. The most obvious use would be to videotape worship services for distribution. Producing service videos not only allows members to review the information, but also is very helpful for reaching shut-ins and those who are homebound. Videotaping special church events such as musicals and dramas is a great way to capture and relive these events. Selling copies of these productions can also be a means of fundraising. (See **Chapter 5** for copyright issues.) Offering video production for weddings is also a valuable service that a church may provide.

Capturing testimonials on tape is another potentially powerful use of videography and has several benefits. Some people may feel more comfortable sharing their stories in front of a camera rather than a large crowd. As people articulate their thoughts, they have the unique opportunity to re-tape any part of the testimony that they would like to clarify. An editor can later insert music and cross-fades to add more emotion to the testimony. The length of the testimony may also be controlled with editing. A properly taped and edited testimonial can have a major impact.

Taking a video camera to the streets and asking people what they think about church or who Jesus was is a great way to bring the community into the church. Conducting these "man-on-the-street" interviews can help keep the congregation from becoming disconnected from their community and unaware of what the average un-churched person thinks regarding religion. The answers to these questions can be very revealing and will hopefully provide motivation to the congregation for reaching out more effectively to the surrounding community. Giving these videos a professional look through editing will give them even more impact.

Other ideas for using video include recording missions updates, building project progress, video skits or vignettes, teacher recruiting, camp recaps...the list of ideas goes on and on. You are only limited by your imagination!

Equipment Checklist

Producing quality video requires a variety of tools. Listed below are items you will need as well as an estimate of basic costs. We will cover each piece of equipment in more detail later.

Equipment	Recommended	Starter
Digital Video Camera	$2000	$ 500
Quality Tripod	$ 450	$ 150
Lighting Kit	$ 400	$ 50
NLE Computer or Standalone	$2000–$4000	$ 800
Audio Equipment	$ 500	$ 50
Total	**$5350**	**$1550**

Video Production Is an Art

As with any art form, video production requires careful attention to detail. There are three areas of video production that are often overlooked:

Lighting. Proper lighting plays a major role in producing great-looking videos. Unfortunately, lighting is usually completely ignored when recording video. Learning some lighting basics will make a big difference.

Camera support. Sometimes the method of supporting the video camera is neglected. The quality of the tripod or other support mechanism can make or break a video production. Most tripods found in department stores are inadequate and should be avoided.

Audio. George Lucas once said that sound quality accounts for at least 50 percent of the overall quality of his *Star Wars* movies. Believe it or not, videos with great sound will actually *look* better!

Attention to these three elements—lighting, camera support, and sound—will enhance the overall quality of your production.

The Production Process

Video production requires a certain amount of preparation. The temptation may be to just pick up a camcorder and start recording, but a well-planned production will be easier to create and will more effectively communicate your message. There are four basic steps in the production process: brainstorming, storyboarding, recording, and editing.

You will first need to determine the main message to be communicated through the production, and then decide what type of video would best convey this message. Members of the production team as well as the vision team should gather for a brainstorming session to determine how the week's theme can best be communicated. For instance, if the theme is "Trusting God," there are several directions that the production could take. If the goal is to explore what most people trust in, the video could be a "man on the street" production asking people, "What do you trust in life?" On the other hand, if one wants to demonstrate the benefits of trusting God, then a testimonial video would be best suited for this task.

Once the goal and type of video is determined, the next step in production would be to storyboard the video. A storyboard is simply a written plan of the production. Storyboards will save time at taping and act as a guide at the editing stage of production. I was once given the task of taping and editing a video to illustrate how my church meets the spiritual needs of children in various stages of life. There were three brothers in the church who were about three years apart in age and who all had similar features. The concept for the video was to show the youngest brother running down a track, have him freeze in mid-air, then have him age by morphing his image into those of his older brothers. The voice-over would talk about our programs for children through youth during each segment. Rather than just winging the video taping, I first developed a storyboard so I had a guide to go by when we met at the track. Developing the storyboard forced me to think creatively as I planned each shot. This preparation also helped me save time as I checked off each shot that needed to be recorded. Having the storyboard also proved to be an invaluable guide when I later edited the footage.

Below is an example of a simple storyboard I developed. A blank storyboard is included on the DVD in the **Video Production Workshop** folder. The file is called *StoryBoard.tif*, and you can print out a copy to use in creating storyboards for your own productions. A storyboard can be simple or complex. There are also some storyboarding programs available for those who are artistically challenged (like me!). The software will automatically put figures into the scene according to the instructions of the director.

Act 1—"Give Me Input!"

Video Cameras

Acquiring a quality video camera is the first step in creating great-looking productions. The final product will not exceed the quality level of the original footage recorded with the camera (garbage in = garbage out). Most consumer cameras process images with only one imaging chip. Although these cameras are usually cheaper in price, they produce video of a much lower quality than what is considered *broadcast quality*. A *three-chip* camera will yield the highest quality results. Three-chip cameras process the colors red, blue, and green separately, resulting in a sharper image and more vibrant colors. Having vivid color is an important consideration since projected video typically loses color. The more color you have to begin with, the better. Three-chip cameras have dropped dramatically in price and now start at less than $2,000.

Regardless of the number of chips, the camera you purchase should record tape digitally. Most digital video cameras at the consumer or prosumer level use the *Mini-DV* format, which is a tape cartridge that resembles a miniature version of a VHS tape. Some consumer video cameras use the *Digital-8* format, which records digital video onto standard Hi-8 tapes. Although these cameras may appear to be similar to a VHS-C or 8mm camera, they record video using a *digital* rather than analog method. Since the video will be edited in the digital realm, it makes sense that the original footage should be acquired digitally. Digital cameras also have a small jack for transferring the digital information to and from computers. This connector is called a FireWire port, and may also be referred to as IEEE-1394 or iLink.

All video cameras feature many automatic functions, such as focus, exposure, and white balance. Because these automatic features may also be an annoyance, you may want to choose a camera that allows the automatic function to be turned off. Cameras are not always as smart as people! Adjusting certain functions manually is a sure way to produce a great-looking image. On that same note, many cameras boast great zoom levels up to 64 to 128 powers or more. The truth is that many cameras have an optical zoom power of only 16 to 24. Anything beyond that is digitally zoomed, and digital zooming almost always looks terrible (similar to digital still cameras, which we discussed in the **Graphics Workshop** section). Turning off the digital zoom feature will help ensure that the picture is always sharp and clear.

Tripods and Camera Support

Though many people spend a great deal of money on a camera, they often attach it to a flimsy tripod. What they end up with is shaky video footage that is distracting and unprofessional despite the great image quality. Quality tripods are rarely found at local electronics franchises. If a tripod costs less than $150, it will likely not meet the standards of professional video. Your local pro camera or video shop, or a mail-order camera company is the best source for finding a quality tripod. One of the main features to look for in a quality tripod is a *fluid head.* But "buyer beware": many inadequate tripods claim that they feature a fluid head. A true fluid head will operate very smoothly with no slack as it pans and tilts the camera. Another important feature to look for in a tripod is solid yet lightweight construction.

In addition to tripods, there are also many other means available for supporting a video camera. Hollywood-style shots may be achieved using dollies, tracks, and cranes. A *dolly* is simply a stand with wheels that is attached to the tripod. It allows you to physically move the tripod while taping. A *track* takes the dolly method one step further, by allowing the dolly to be guided along a set of rails. Using a *crane*, the camera can be lifted high into the air to create dramatic and professional-looking shots. The *Steadicam®*, which is a camera support system that is worn like a harness, is another example of a support device. The camera is attached to this device and "floats" on the support. In recent years, low-budget versions of the *Steadicam,* have been designed for smaller cameras. In addition to these support devices there are attachments for cars, helmets—and just about anything. You could even use a wheelchair as a makeshift dolly. Not only do these tools give video a polished look, they also tend to expand the limits of creativity and spark new ideas.

Audio Equipment

As we mentioned earlier, adding quality audio to video productions is often neglected. Although we can only scratch the surface of this complex subject here, I do want to offer a few basic equipment and recording suggestions. The on-board microphones on most camcorders are inadequate. When producing "man-on-the-street" interviews, a handheld microphone should be used. This will help with clarity and keep out background noise. Some microphones are designed to connect directly to the camcorder's microphone input. There are also adapters for camcorders that will allow virtually any standard microphone to be used. For testimonials, it is recommended to use lavaliere microphones. Lavaliere microphones will make the audio recorded more intelligible because they are worn on the lapel and closer to the person speaking. An audio mixer may be required in some instances where multiple microphones are used. When recording a musical, it is best to place several microphones around the room as well as tapping into the church soundboard. Using headphones, an audio technician can mix a balance between the live sound and the feed from the church mixer.

Act 2—"Let There Be Light"

Though often overlooked, quality lighting is probably the most crucial element required for making great-looking video. Without proper lighting, subjects look flat and unattractive, colors are not reproduced accurately, and image graininess is increased. Using proper lighting separates the amateurs from the pros.

The basic lighting method, called *3-point lighting*, consists of using a trio of lights to illuminate a scene: a *key light,* a *fill light*, and a *backlight*. The *key light*, usually the brightest, is positioned in front and to the side of the subject being taped. The *fill light* is offset opposite the key light. Less bright than the key light, the fill light helps diminish the shadows created by the key light. Finally, the *backlight*, located behind the subject, helps define shape and create depth. An example of how a backlight functions can be seen in situations where the outline of a person wearing black can be clearly seen even though the person is against a black background. Even big-budget movie sets start off with this basic lighting method.

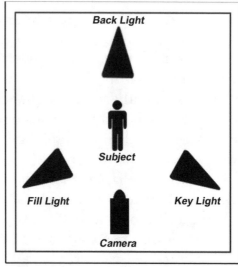

Basic 3-Point Lighting

To make it easier to set up and use proper lighting, I highly recommend buying a lighting kit. These kits include the proper type of lights as well as adjustable stands for them. Most also come with a case to house and transport the lights and stands. There is a wide variety of choices and prices for lighting kits, and they may be found at pro video shops and mail-order companies. While some built-in lights on a camera can help with lighting, a 3-point lighting kit is a must-have for producing high-quality videos. If you cannot afford a lighting kit, you can construct one using work lights from a hardware store. These are the bright halogen lights you might use when painting a room. Many come with their own stands and some come with clamps for attaching the lights to almost anything.

Experimenting is the best way to master lighting. Have someone sit on a couch and read a book while you try different lighting positions and intensities. Write down the positions of your lights as you videotape the subject. This is a great way to understand the nuances of lighting and how your camera reacts to different lighting situations.

Act 3—The Shootout

Most people are familiar with the image of a director using his hands to "frame" a shot in a movie. This is actually a useful technique and will help the director visualize what the final product will look like on a screen. *Framing* and composition are very important aspects of creating quality productions. There are a variety of framing techniques. The next time you watch a movie or television show or a commercial, pay close attention to the camera angles and where the main focus of attention is on the screen. Try mimicking some of these techniques as you prepare your storyboard and shoot the video.

Some basic camera techniques are listed in **Appendix M**. One of my favorite techniques is the *point of view* shot. This simple method will spice up any production. For example, if the person being videotaped is looking out a window, cut to a shot aimed out the window for a moment and then back to the person. This will show the viewer the perspective of the subject, allowing them to "see" what the subject sees. Creating effective video is all about adding details like this.

Act 4—Making Magic: Nonlinear Video Editing

Editing video is my favorite part of the production process. In the past, video editing usually required expensive equipment, involving multiple tape recorders and mixing equipment. It was a time-consuming and labor-intensive process. Today, almost any church can afford editing equipment that will yield high-quality video productions. What used to take a whole room full of equipment can now be accomplished with one computer. Editing video on a computer is referred to as *nonlinear editing* (or *NLE*). The term "nonlinear" refers to the fact that a computer is not limited to the linear limitations of tape. Video clips captured into a NLE computer may be accessed randomly and reused in a number of different ways without any signal loss or degradation.

Many turnkey NLE computer systems are available on the market today, or one may be custom built. Most off-the-shelf computers are difficult to configure for nonlinear editing, though the expandability and compatibility of these machines are improving. The computer specifications that we discussed in **Chapter 2** are also very relevant to an NLE computer, though having a fast processor speed is generally more important in an editing computer. The most recent video computer hardware devices rely heavily on processor speed for maximum functionality. For instance, the editing ability of some recent editing cards improves with faster processors. In other words, faster processors will allow the editing hardware to do more. Another prime consideration in an NLE computer is the hard drive capacity. Digital video takes up five megabytes of hard drive space for every minute of recorded video. Large capacity drives are very affordable and a must for an editing computer. A standard IDE ATA-100 drive spinning at 7,200 RPM is more than adequate for digital video editing. The drive for video should be set up as a separate, dedicated drive for best results.

The heart of a video-editing computer is the video capture card. The capture card acts as an interface between the camera or VCR and the computer. It digitizes the footage and saves it to the computer hard drive. There are many varieties of capture cards available at varying levels of quality and features. In general, the price of a capture device is usually indicative of its abilities and value of its bundled software.

As we mentioned earlier, many digital video cameras feature a FireWire connector. Most capture cards include a FireWire connector as well, allowing the camera and computer to interface with each other. A FireWire cable carries the video footage in a digital format (simply called Digital Video or DV). The cable is bi-directional and transfers the video and audio information to and from the computer and the camcorder. Traditional analog video requires up to six cables (one video and two audio for both input and output), whereas a FireWire cable carries all of this information along one cable in both directions. Since it is digital information, there is virtually no signal degradation. Some capture cards also contain standard analog inputs and outputs in addition to the FireWire connector, which is handy for capturing footage from a VCR.

The software bundled with a capture card can often be just as valuable (and sometimes more valuable) than the card itself. For instance, the most popular program for video editing is Adobe® Premiere®, which currently retails for $550. The full version of Premiere comes bundled with many cards, including the some that are in the $300 price range. The benefits of spending a bit more on a card for its software bundle quickly become obvious. Capture cards in the $1,000 price range offer even more software and benefits. For example, in addition to Premiere, many mid-priced cards include DVD authoring software, music software, and extra video effects. However, their cost-benefit is even more apparent in its hardware abilities, which enable them to perform many *real-time* effects.

Whenever two captured video clips are combined—in a cross-fade transition, for example—most capture card hardware will require that the transition be rendered. That is, the computer will calculate each frame where the two clips intersect to create a new video file. This, of course, takes time and computer resources. The more complicated the transition, the longer it will take to render the effect. A *real-time* capture card will perform transitions, effects, and graphic overlays without the need to first render them. Real-time capture hardware will dramatically speed up the time it takes to edit video productions. The price difference between a $100 FireWire card and a $1,000 real-time capture card is well worth the money considering the time saved, better quality video produced, and amount of bundled software included. Some recommended companies that manufacture real-time cards are listed in **Appendix N**.

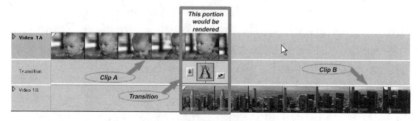

A - B Editing

There are a number of real-time cards available from various companies. As you consider which model to purchase, pay strict attention to the system recommendations that the company specifies for its hardware and make sure that your computer meets or exceeds these recommendations. Video editing puts a great deal of strain on a computer and can make it temperamental. Also be sure to read the fine print to determine exactly what a real-time card can actually perform without rendering. Not everything can be accomplished in real time with every card. There will inevitably be some rendering required in more complicated projects.

These capture cards may also be purchased in turnkey computer systems. This is a great alternative for media ministries that are not comfortable configuring their own systems. A turnkey system is built specifically for video editing and tested with the most compatible hardware for the capture card being used in the system. Although they cost more, turnkey video editing systems are designed for maximum performance with minimal hassle.

Another option for editing would be to purchase a stand-alone nonlinear video editor. Sometimes called "video-editing appliances," these units do only one thing: edit video. They are very easy to use and require little training. Although they usually have fewer features than a computer-based editing system, they do include the basic tools needed for video editing. Stand-alone editors work very much like a VCR and are designed with ease-of-use in mind. A media ministry wanting to start a video ministry without a great deal of effort should look into video editing appliances. (See **Appendix N** for a listing of available vendors.)

The Editing Process

Capturing

Capturing the raw footage or unedited video material to the computer hard drive is the initial step in the nonlinear editing process. First, connect the camera to the capture card via a FireWire cable. Many capture cards include a video capture program designed specifically for that card and include some advanced features. The software allows you to not only transfer the video and audio information via the FireWire cable but also to control the camcorder. With one press of a button, the program will rewind the Mini DV tape in the camcorder and capture the entire tape in real time. The program will detect when the camera was started and stopped and create a separate video file for each clip. The clips may then be quickly renamed for organization, and unwanted clips easily deleted.

Capture cards that do not include a software capture utility can capture footage through Premiere's built-in capture feature, which is very intuitive and has VCR-like controls. If the footage being captured comes from an analog source, such as a VCR, the capture process is not automatic as described above. Since the source device cannot be controlled by the program (because it is not FireWire), the capture process must be started manually by clicking the **Record** button in Premiere after pressing **Play** on the VCR or camcorder. Pressing **Escape (ESC)** on the keyboard will stop the capturing.

Editing

Once all of the raw footage has been captured and transferred to the computer, you no longer need the camcorder. This could give someone else an opportunity to start another video project while the current project is being edited. The video exercise on the DVD goes into detail on how to edit clips using Adobe Premier, so we will not cover this information here. Since video production and editing is such a wide topic, some additional recommended reading is listed in **Appendix P**.

Rendering and Exporting

As we have already discussed, the amount of rendering time required during editing depends on the hardware being used. Even with the best real-time capture cards, some rendering may be required. Fortunately, the days of waiting all night for a project to render are over. Usually the edits will be completed within minutes. Projects that include a great deal of layering, graphics, and complex transitions could take as long as several hours depending on the overall length of the video.

Once all rendering has been completed, the video needs to be exported from the computer. Although the video may be played back from the computer through Premiere, the video information naturally cannot remain on the computer forever. The hard drive will eventually need to be freed up for other projects. There are also some concerns about playing the video from the computer during a service. Though the computer may perform flawlessly fifty times in a row, the possibility of encountering a glitch on Sunday morning always exists. Therefore, I recommend using a more dependable playback source. Here are some options for the video's final destination:

Export back to Mini DV. The simplest way to archive a completed video project is to record the finished project back to tape. By using the "Print to Video" feature in Premiere, the video will automatically be recorded back to the camcorder via FireWire. The video may be then played back from the camcorder and stored for future use. Since FireWire is used, virtually no signal loss occurs during the transfer.

Create a DVD. DVD burners have become very affordable in recent months. Many capture cards include software for creating a DVD complete with menus, and are very easy to use. The edited video must first be rendered into a format that the authoring software can recognize. The native format for DVD is called MPEG-2. This rendering process can take anywhere from minutes to hours, depending on the computer hardware and length of the video. Once it is in the MPEG-2 format, the material can then be "authored" using the DVD software and burned to a writable DVD (DVD-R). Most current DVD players will be able to read DVD-R and the video can then be archived and played back from a standard DVD player.

Export to MPEG-1. Exporting your video in MPEG-1 format produces lower-quality video that can be played back from within PowerPoint and some worship software. This option is generally undesirable for archiving since it degrades the video quality. However, since it will yield a smaller file size, MPEG-1 files work better for web use, allow for easy access from within PowerPoint, and may also fit on a standard writable CD-ROM.

Export for web-streaming. In addition to MPEG-1, there are a couple of other formats suitable for posting to a website. The most common are QuickTime,® Windows® Media Player, and RealPlayer® formats. Projects can be converted to one of these formats using Premiere 6.5 (or a plug-in for older versions of Premiere) or other stand-alone programs. These programs will usually walk the user through choosing options for quality level and video size. Naturally, higher-quality video files will be larger, which is undesirable for websites.[11] The three main formats mentioned above require that the person browsing the site have a player that will read the video file. Most browser software will have the plug-ins for these players already included, and those that do not may easily download the free players so that the videos may be viewed.

Top Ten Editing Tips

1. Transitions

Most capture cards come bundled with a surplus of fancy, high-tech transitions. The temptation is to pack a video project with these cool features to show off what can be done. It is important to remember that 99.9 percent of all transitions are cuts; that is, no transition at all. Cross-fades are the next most commonly used transition. Fades should be used during video pieces involving emotion and soft music, such as testimonials. The more fantastic, 3-D-type effects are perfect for introducing or exiting a video piece. These exciting transitions may also be used more liberally for youth-oriented videos.

2. Titles and Text

Using text not only helps make the viewer aware of the title of a video or the name of a person, it can also reinforce the message of the video. For instance, if a testimonial video emphasizes trust in God and the interviewee uses the word "faith" in a sentence, an effective editing method would be to fade the word "faith" into the frame for a moment. This underscores the theme of the testimony and the topic for the day and helps the viewer focus on the main points of the testimony.

3. 3-D Animation

We have become accustomed to the professional 3-D effects seen on television programs such as newscasts and sporting events. However, creating 3-D animation cannot be learned overnight; It can take years of training to truly master the art of 3-D. There are, however, several programs with automated "wizards" that will walk a user through the process of animating text and 3-D objects. These programs can help add professional flavor to a video project with minimal effort. So, while it may not be possible to become

The Video effects tab in Premiere reveals folders with various effects that may be simply dragged onto a clip.

the next Phil Vischer (computer animator and creator of VeggieTales) overnight, one can create some simple 3-D animations with minimal effort.

4. Colorizing and Distorting Video

"Treating" footage with a color or distortion provides another way to spice up a video. For instance, an editor could use the *color balance* video filter to tint a portion of video to any color. This interesting technique will add personality to a video and works particularly well with "man-on-the-street" videos.

Video may also be distorted in a variety of ways for interesting effects. Most of these filters may be found under the **Video** tab in Premiere. You should simply experiment with the **Distort** and **Perspective** effects available in Premiere to understand how each of these filters affects your video.

5. Moving and Resizing

Video can be rotated and resized using one of the **Perspective** effects available in Premiere. The video may also be moved around the frame, creating interesting effects. To access this feature, right-click the clip you would like to manipulate, choose **Video Options,** and then **Motion**.

Using the motion settings, the clip may be moved around the screen, rotated, resized, and distorted.

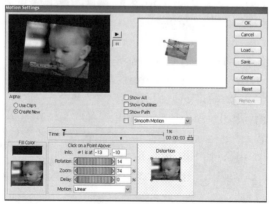

6. Bluescreening or Keying

The technique used to display a map behind a weather person involves having the person stand in front of a blue screen. This technique is referred to as *keying*, because the color blue is *keyed* out to reveal the graphic of the map. This is actually a fairly simple process. To make this effect hassle-free, be sure that the color background behind the subject is evenly lit. This will make the keying process easier for Premiere. The video to be shown behind the subject in front of the blue-screen should be placed on the *Video 2* track above the *Video A* track. Right-click the video on the *Video 2* track and select **Video Options** and then **Transparency** from the menu. Under **Key Options**, select the appropriate type (usually color-key) and make adjustments until the desired effect is accomplished. This technique will probably make more sense to you after completing the DVD exercise. You can also use this method to create a glowing effect for angels by using a yellow cloth behind a person in an angel costume. Using the color-key effect and a picture of stars, experiment with the adjustments until a soft halo effect surrounds the person.

7. Stock Footage and Animations

An entire production can be created even if you don't own a camcorder. Using stock footage and animations combined with text, music, and voice-overs, professional videos may be put together with minimal effort. **Appendix O** lists several sources for purchasing footage and animations for editing. Several samples of these types of products are included on the DVD.

8. Voiceovers

Every church has at least one person with a very interesting and professional voice. They most likely do not even realize it. Wander around during church fellowships or other church events and try to locate this person. Having someone for narration and voiceovers really helps take your production to a higher level. When recording, keep in mind that people tend to "drop off" the end of their sentences. Act as a vocal coach and help your readers keep their volume, pacing, and enthusiasm consistent throughout the whole recording.

9. Background Music

Adding background music provides the "finishing touch" that will bring a production to life. Choose your music carefully and be sure not to violate copyright laws. There are literally hundreds of sources for royalty-free music (see **Appendix Q**). There are two main things to keep in mind when selecting and adding background music. First, avoid music with vocals if any other talking is involved in the video segment because this makes it difficult for the listener to distinguish between the lyrics and what is being spoken. Second, adjust the volume of the background music to a *lower* level than what you (the editor) are comfortable with. Because it is difficult to discern the appropriate volume level when you are editing, set the level a little lower than what "sounds right." This will most likely be the best volume level.

10. Sound Effects

Hundreds of detailed sound effects are added to a movie production during editing. Adding subtle sound effects to a church video production can make it come alive. For instance, if you are shooting a segment in a park, add some birds or children laughing in the background. Incorporating these details will give a professional flair to a production. It can be a lot of fun and does not take much time. Sound effect CDs may be purchased at almost any music store.

Premiere Basics

Below are a few basic steps for getting started with Adobe Premiere:

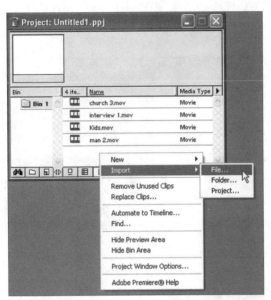

The first step after capturing footage is to import elements for editing into the project bin. Right-click in the bin area and choose **Import**. You may then navigate to the desired files, folder or project and bring it in for editing.

Next, double-click a clip in the bin to "trim" the parts of the video that you do not need. Click the desired starting point and ending point, and the rest of the clip will be ignored. Note that the original clip will not be permanently changed and may still be manipulated again for a different purpose. Once trimmed, the clip may then be dragged onto the timeline on either video track A or video track B.

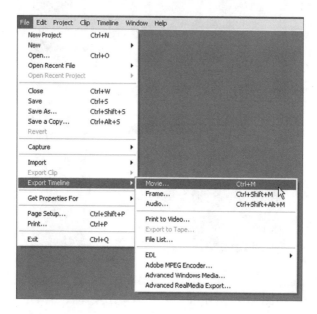

Finally, export the footage to a new file for playback, DVD authoring, or posting to the Internet. Note the options for MPEG, Windows Media, or RealMedia, all formats that are great for website use.

Endnotes

[1] One such debate can be read in ChurchMedia.net's online community archives.

[2] According to an online poll at ChurchMedia.net, 75% of the people involved in the media ministry of churches worldwide are volunteers. Only 10% are paid as full-time media ministers and another 15% on staff have other duties besides media.

[3] I use this term with love and affection since I consider myself one of these! Embrace your geekiness!

[4] An informal poll at ChurchMedia.net showed that nearly 65% of people preparing media receive their material two days or less before a service and 22% have up to five days.

[5] In fact, according to a ChurchMedia.net poll most people do not get their material until two days before a service. Our polls also show that almost half of media ministers only spend two to five hours preparing media.

[6] Data based on an ongoing informal survey at ChurchMedia.net.

[7] It is not necessary to upgrade to Windows XP to run PowerPoint XP, although the Windows XP platform has many advantages for media ministries. Windows 98 or better is recommended.

[8] In the ChurchMedia.net community archives you will find an interesting thread on this question of when to advance to the next slide during a song.

[9] A ChurchMedia.net poll shows that in only 16% of churches using media do most people pay attention to the announcements.

[10] I designed a graphics collection called *Kick Starters Background Sets* specifically for this purpose (similar packages are available from other companies as well). My theme-sets include several types of backgrounds.

[11] However, according to research at ChurchMedia.net, web users with high-speed Internet access are on the rise, making the larger file sizes less of an issue.

Appendices

Appendix A

GO W I D E!

Keep a close eye on your televisions and computer monitors. The day is fast approaching when you will notice a strange phenomenon: the screens you stare at day in and day out will start to s t r e t c h! The advent of HDTV and the convergence of media distribution will make the widescreen format a standard. Sooner or later all image displays will have an aspect ratio of 16 by 9, including the projection screens found in churches. At present, most screens have an aspect ratio of 4:3. This means that a projection screen that measures 9 feet by 12 feet will stretch to 9 feet by 16 feet. Of course, these screens are not going to grow by themselves. They will eventually need to be replaced with wider screens. Don't run out to your favorite video dealer right away, however. It will be years before a widescreen becomes an absolute necessity. But if you want to take advantages of the widescreen format right away, there is no real reason to wait. If you are planning to build a new facility with a projection system, you should definitely consider going W I D E!

To understand widescreens, you must comprehend how the original material for widescreen is created. Movies to be shown in a movie theatre are filmed in widescreen format. When renting a video, you may have noticed a message at the beginning of a movie that says, "This movie has been modified from its original format to fit your screen." When the movie was transferred to video, the original film was manipulated to fit the size of a television. Some parts of the movie may be "artificially" panned from side to side so the viewer will not miss any action that does not fit on a standard television screen. This is called "Pan and Scan." Everything outside this window is then cropped off so that the image will fill a standard 4:3 aspect ratio television screen. The viewer will not experience the movie as it was originally intended because almost a third of the original image is missing. Serious movie buffs and DVD enthusiasts will therefore opt for the "letterbox" format when watching movies on tape or disc. This method adds a black border at the top and bottom of a standard 4:3 screen to achieve the original 16:9 aspect ratio. Many video cameras will also create the letterbox for 16:9 videotaping, which would allow a letterbox image to be projected on a 16:9 screen using a standard projector. The black portions of the image would overshoot the screen and hardly be noticed.

Letterboxing involves taking a widescreen image and reducing in proportion to fit a 4:3 display, leaving a black border at the top and bottom. "Pan and scan" is the cropping method described earlier. Either option is not the most desirable, and ultimately both methods will become obsolete. The problem is that the size of the original source material does not match the size of the output display device. At present, most television programs are videotaped in 4:3 formats. All of the equipment used to produce the programs is designed for 4:3. This, too, is changing. Ultimately, all original material will be created in the 16:9 format, meaning that your favorite sitcom will get wider as your television also stretches. This also means that the equipment used to create the programs needs to be 16:9 compatible. Many television stations and studios will need to upgrade their equipment to comply with the new standard. Projectors, cameras, and playback devices with native 16:9 capabilities will become more prevalent and affordable, thus allowing churches to also "keep up with the times." Many manufacturers are adding native 16:9 product lines at the 1366 x 768 resolution while most screen manufacturers have had 16:9 aspect ratio screens available for years.

So far we have discussed video and film output in the 16:9 format. Most churches will be mainly interested in widescreen computer output. Again, there are two ways of accomplishing a 16:9 format. The first is to "letterbox" your slides in PowerPoint. Under **File > Page** setup the height of the slides may be reduced to create this effect. When the presentation is shown on a 16:9 screen, the black bars at the top and bottom will overshoot the screen and the slide will fill the widescreen area. The second and more desirable method is to use a graphics card capable of 16:9 output and a projector with a native 16:9 display. At present, XGA resolution is 1024 x 768. Widescreen XGA is 1366 x 768. A projector with a native resolution of 1366 x 768 combined with a computer equipped with a graphics card capable of 1366 x 768 output will result in a complete 16:9 system.

One of the biggest motivations for going wide is the advantage that a 16:9 screen provides for laying out text. Rather than having to split sentences into two lines, song lyrics may be displayed a full sentence at a time. Full verses and choruses will fit on a single 16:9 slide without having to break them into multiple slides. (See examples below in **Figure 1** and **2**.)

All hail the pow'r
of Jesus' name,
Let angels prostrate fall,
Let angels prostrate fall,
Bring forth the royal
diadem.

Figure 1

This is really only half of a verse and does not really flow with the music.

Now look at the whole verse on a 16 x 9 screen:

> All hail the pow'r of Jesus' name,
>
> Let angels prostrate fall,
>
> Let angels prostrate fall,
>
> Bring forth the royal diadem.
>
> And crown Him, crown Him,
>
> Crown Him, crown Him,
>
> And crown Him Lord of all.

Figure 2

What a difference! Now the whole verse may be displayed without having to break up the lines.

Equipment Considerations for Widescreen

The benefits of using widescreens in the church will become more evident as churches find creative ways to implement them. There are a number of larger churches already using 16:9 displays. Within the next five to ten years there will be a growing number of smaller to midsize churches that will add widescreens to their ministries. There will come a day that *all* churches using projection systems will need to convert to 16:9. Church leaders with vision and foresight will strongly consider going wide as soon as possible. Who knows? Perhaps your church will help start a new trend and change public perception of the church: The church could become known as being *ahead* of the times!

Reasons to Go WIDE

- Eventually we will be a widescreen society.

- Widescreen equipment is becoming more affordable and more prevalent.

- Song lyrics may be displayed in a more logical manner.

- Side-by-side displays of video and computer information allow for greater flexibility in communicating messages.

- It would make you the coolest church around!

Appendix B

No Room for Traditional Worship Anymore?

A friend and I once had an online debate on Ginghamsburg's media ministry forum about traditional worship. My friend made a very bold statement, saying that he did not see the need for any traditional style worship services anymore. I have always had strong convictions about this, so I stepped up to the plate to present my views. I argued that there are two big reasons to continue traditional worship: my mom and my dad. In a traditional service that would put me to sleep, I look at my mom and she is worshiping God like nobody's business. But when my mom attends a Gen-X style service where I am thriving in worship, she wants to run, duck, and cover! God made all of us with unique personalities and tastes. Just because we feel that a certain way of conducting a service is out of date does not mean that it should be doomed to extinction. Remember that the senior members of a church should be respected and not ignored. Many older members are the cornerstones of a church. In fact, they may just be ones who pay for the equipment for the media ministry! Many churches that face potential problems with seniors will start a contemporary service to be held at a different time from the traditional service. This is a great idea and will give everyone the option to worship in an environment that is best suited for her or him. If a separate traditional service is to be held, as much effort should be exerted for this service as for the contemporary service. The traditional service deserves just as much attention to detail as the contemporary service. The danger of splintering the church by segregating the congregation should be avoided by occasionally having joint services with a "blended" style. This will give a unique opportunity for both groups to experience a taste of each type of worship.

Appendix C

DYS Video Stage Monitors

Song lyrics generated by worship software or PowerPoint and displayed on a large screen through the projector cannot be seen by those on the stage, leaving them oblivious to what the congregation sees. For instance, you may have noticed in a service that some of the choir members on stage are not in sync with everyone else. For this reason, many churches have installed video stage monitors. Just as audio stage monitors have become a vital part of a sound system, video monitor play an important role in a video system

Building a video monitoring system is fairly inexpensive and easy to put together. The components needed should be available locally. Select one or more televisions that have at least a 25" screen. The *RF modulator, RF amplifier / splitter*, and *coaxial cable* you will need should be available at a local electronics store like Radio Shack. The *scan converter* can be found at most computer stores or ordered online.

How It Works

Duplicating the image seen on the big screen to the video monitor involves a couple of signal conversions. The *scan converter* transforms the computer signal into an image that a TV can display. The *RF modulator* converts the output of the scan converter to a signal that can run through a long cable and be split into several signals, which in turn can be displayed through the standard coaxial inputs of a TV.

Connections

The graphics output on your computer is usually connected to your projector through a long cable. Take that cable and connect it to the **Monitor Out** port on the scan converter. (It may also be labeled **Thru** or **Loop**.) Using the short VGA cable supplied with the scan converter, connect the monitor output on your computer to the input of the scan converter. Using a composite video cable, connect the video output from the scan converter to the input of the RF modulator. Connect the long coaxial cable to the output of the RF modulator and run it to the input of the RF amplifier/splitter. Finally, connect the outputs of the splitter to the coaxial inputs of the televisions, using the shorter coaxial cables.

Build cabinets for the televisions to give them a finished look. You might want to use the same type of carpet or finish as your audio monitors.

Another solution is to place a large mirror in front of the stage and teach your worship team to read backwards. However, I would suggest building this video monitor system to keep your choir on cue.

Appendix D

Technology & Media Magazines Specifically for Churches

(All prices are in US dollars and subject to change.)

NRB (National Religious Broadcasters)
www.nrb.org
703-330-7000
Free subscription

Church Business Magazine
www.churchbusiness.com
480-990-1101
1 Year (6 Issues): $24.95

Church Production Magazine
www.churchproduction.com
919-677-4000
Free subscription for US and Canada

Church & Worship Technology Magazine
craig@workhorsepublishing.com
Fax: 480-585-0456
Free subscription (12 issues per year)

Christian Computing Magazine
www.ccmag.com
800-456-1868
1 Year (11 Issues): $19.95
2 Years (22 Issues): $34.95

Technologies for Worship Magazine
www.tfwm.com
905-473-9822
1 Year (6 Issues): $29.95
2 Year (12 Issues): $49.95

Your Church Magazine
www.christianitytoday.com/yc
800-632-2738
Free Subscription (6/Year)

Appendix E

Media Training Specifically for Churches

(All prices are in US dollars and subject to change.)

Note: This list does not include audio training, nor does it include conferences that have media tracks. It only includes conferences dedicated exclusively to media.

Digital Storytellers—Len Wilson and Jason Moore
www.midnightoilproductions.net
One-day events at various locations around the US
$89/first person, $69 each additional

Inspiration Conference—*Technologies for Worship Magazine*
www.tfwm.com
905-473-9822
An annual one-week event with over 100 sessions
Prices vary, based on programs, etc.

Lumicon Institute
www.lumicon.org
866-LUMICON (toll-free)
A year-long certificate program in "Digital Culture Ministry"
$1,995 Tuition

Media Ministry Made Easy—Tim Eason
www.churchmedia.net
800-220-2923
One-day seminar and workshop in various locations in the US and Canada
$99/person. Group rates available.

National Religious Broadcasters Convention
www.nrb.org
703-330-7000
An annual one-week event focusing mainly on broadcasting

Prices range from $70 to $525 based on programs, etc.

Appendix F

Training Events & Magazines
(Not Church-specific)

Infocomm
www.icia.org
800-659-7469
Projection and display systems
training and trade show

**NAB—National Association
of Broadcasters**
www.nab.org
202-429-5300
The biggest annual convention
on video, audio, and lighting
technology.

**Computer VideoMaker
Magazine**
www.videomaker.com
800-284-3226
13 Issues: $14.97

DV Magazine
www.dv.com
888-776-7002
12 Issues: $19.99

Presentations Magazine
www.presentations.com
847-647-7987
Free subscription

Videography Magazine
www.videography.com
323-634-3400
Free subscription

**Digital Publishing Design
Graphics**
www.designgraphics.com.au
800-688-6247
12 Issues: $69

Computer Graphics World
http://cgw.pennet.com
(847) 559-7500
Free subscription

Photoshop User
www.photoshopuser.com
800-738-8513
$99 Annual Membership Fee

Appendix G

Copyright Websites

Christian Copyright Licensing International:
www.ccli.com

Christian Video Licensing Inc: www.cvli.org

Church Copyright Administration:
www.churchca.com

Copyright and Fair Use, Stanford University Libraries: http://fairuse.stanford.edu

Microsoft: www.microsoft.com/permission

Motion Picture Licensing Corporation: www.mplc.com

US Copyright Office: www.loc.gov/copyright

Appendix H

Quick Tips on Movie Clips

Movies have become an integral part of our society and are very influential. Using a movie clip to illustrate a point is a fantastic way to communicate in a way that almost anyone can relate to. Here are three tips to help maximize the use of movie clips:

Choose your movie carefully. As we mentioned, the media being used should not compromise the Word. There are many movies that can have a great impact when used cautiously. There are others that should not be used at all. If a clip from a questionable movie is being shown, be sure to add a disclaimer. For instance, "We are showing this clip because it does a great job of illustrating our point, but we don't recommend that you rent it as it contains...." I have seen some churches print this type of disclaimer in their bulletin, which is a good idea. Remember that when a movie is shown during a service, the church indirectly endorses that film. Clarifying the church's stance on a movie will help avoid misunderstandings.

Keep it short. The length of the clip should be limited to one to three minutes. Longer sequences will become more of a distraction than an enhancement. Before showing the clip, it is helpful to "set up" the scene by giving some background on what is happening in the movie. This will also help cut down on the length of the clip.

Make your point stick. On more than one occasion I have seen a pastor show a movie clip and then say something to the effect of, "Wasn't that a relevant parable?" The problem is that the clip was never referred to again. The next time I saw the movie I remembered that a clip was shown in church, but still could not remember the sermon or how the movie applied to it. Make sure to refer to the clip or a character in a movie several times during the sermon. The reason for showing a movie clip is this: the next time a person sees that movie, they should recall the sermon and how it applies to their lives

Using these tips for showing movie clips will help ensure their effectiveness.

Appendix I

Release Form for Video Productions

Individual Release Agreement

The undersigned enter into an Agreement with Video/Audio Media Production as representatives for _____. I have been informed and understand that Video/Audio Media Production is producing a videotape program on location and that my name, likeness, image, voice, appearance, and performance is being recorded and made a part of the production.

I grant **Video/Audio Media Production** and its designees the right to use my name, likeness, voice, appearance, and performance as embodied in the Product whether recorded on or transferred to videotape, film slides, photographs, audio-tapes, or other media not now known or later developed. This grant includes without limitation the right to edit mix or duplicate and to use or re-use the product in whole or in part as Video/Audio Media Production may elect. **Video/Audio Media Production** or its designee shall have complete owner-ship of the Product in which I appear, including copyright interests and I acknowledge that I have no interest or ownership in the Product or its copyright.

I also grant **Video/Audio Media Production** and its designees the right to broadcast, exhibit, market, sell and otherwise distribute the Product, either in whole or in parts and either alone or with other products for commercial or non-commercial television or theater, closed-circuit exhibition, home video dis-tribution or any other purpose that **Video/Audio Media Production** or its designees in their sole discretion may determine. This grant includes the right to use the Product for promoting or publicizing any of the uses.

I confirm that I have the right to enter into this Agreement, that I am not restricted by any commitments to third parties. I hereby give all clearances, copyright, and otherwise for the use of my name, likeness, image, voice, appear-ance, and performance embodied in the Product. I expressly release and indem-nify **Video/Audio Media Production** and its officers, employees, agents, and designees from any and all claims known or unknown arising out of or in any way connected with the above granted uses and representations. The rights granted **Video/Audio Media Production** herein are perpetual and worldwide.

In consideration of all the above, I hereby acknowledge receipt of reasonable and fair consideration from **Video/Audio Media Production**.

I have read the foregoing and understand its terms and stipulations and agree to all of them.

Print Name_____

Signature_____

Address (City, State, Zip)_____

Social Security #_____

Date_____

Program Name_____

* More forms may be found at www.videouniversity.com/releases.htm

165

Appendix J

Recommended Graphics Resources

Religious:

GoodSalt—www.goodsalt.com
Kick Starters*—www.kickstarters.net
The Media Collection*—www.themediacollection.com
Midnight Oil Productions—
                 www.midnightoilproductions.net
Parting Water*—www.partingwater.com
Visual Worship*—www.visualworship.com
WorshipBacks*—www.worshipbacks.com
Worship Photos*—www.worshipphotos.com

General:

AbleStock—www.ablestock.com
Comstock—www.comstock.com
Corbis—www.bizpresenter.com
Digital Juice—www.digitaljuice.com
FotoSearch—www.fotosearch.com

Free Samples of these resources are on the DVD in the **Bonus Resources** *folder!*

Appendix K

Most Used Shortcut Keys

General Windows Shortcuts

ALT + Tab: Switch between open applications.

Ctrl + Tab: Switch between open documents.

Windows + E: Start Windows Explorer.

Windows + M: Minimize all open Windows.

Windows + F: Find a file.

ALT + F4: Close current Window.

Ctrl + C: Copy something to the clipboard.

Ctrl + V: Paste from the clipboard.

Ctrl + X: Cut something (puts it on the clipboard).

Ctrl + N: Create a new file.

Ctrl + O: Open a file.

Ctrl + S: Save a file.

Ctrl + Z: Undo an action.

Ctrl + Y: Redo an action.

Print Screen: Copy a picture of the screen to the clipboard.

Alt + Print Screen: Copy a picture of the selected window to the clipboard.

Esc: Cancel a menu or dialog box action.

PowerPoint Shortcuts

F5: Start a presentation.

F6: Move between panes.

Ctrl + D: Make a copy of the selected slide.

Right Arrow, Down Arrow, Spacebar or Mouse Click: Perform next animation or advance to next slide.

Left Arrow, Up Arrow: Perform previous animation or return to previous slide.

Number + Enter: Jump to the slide *number*.

B or Period: Toggle between black screen/un-black screen.

Esc: End slide show.

Ctrl + H: Hide the mouse pointer and navigation button immediately.

Photoshop Shortcuts (See page 92 for toolbar shortcuts)

Enter: Complete the edit (crop, transform, etc.)

Arrow Keys: Nudge the position of a layer by 1 pixel in any direction.

Ctrl + T: Free Transform

Shift + Ctrl + N: New Layer

Ctrl + J: Copy Layer

Double-click a layer: Open Layer Effects

Ctrl + D: Deselect Layer

Shift + Ctrl + I: Invert the Selection

Alt + Ctrl + D: Feather Selection

Ctrl + +: Zoom In

Ctrl + - : Zoom Out

Premiere (Premiere has a TON of shortcuts! Explore the program for more.)

V: Selection Tool

M: Range Selection Tools (toggle)

C: Razor Tools (toggle)

U: Fade Adjustment Tools/Link Tool (toggle)

N: Mark In/Mark Out

Ctrl + / (Backslash): New Bin

Ctrl + I: Import a file.

Ctrl + M: Export timeline to a movie.

Ctrl + Shift + V: Paste to fit.

Ctrl + Alt + V: Paste attributes

Ctrl + Shift + /: Duplicate clip

Ctrl + B: Clip transparency

Ctrl + Y: Clip motion

Enter: Preview/Render

Appendix L

Worship Software Companies

EasyWorship*
Softouch Development, Inc.
www.easyworship.com
918-250-1493

MediaShout*
MediaComplete Corporation
www.mediashout.com
888-829-7168

Presentation Manager
Creative Lifestyles, Inc.
www.presentationmanager.info
248-685-8179

Prologue Sunday Plus*
Grass Roots Software
www.sundayplus.com
877-274-7277

SongShow Plus
R-Technics Inc.
www.songshowplus.com
888-225-8054

WorshipBuilder*
DOnline Inc.
www.worshipbuilder.com
877-690-4460

Worship Him!
Freedom Software
www.worship-him.com

* *Demo versions are available on the DVD.*

Appendix M

Camera Techniques

Pan: A camera move that pivots the camera horizontally—right to left or left to right—from a stationary position. Use this technique to follow one subject to another, show relationships between subjects, or scan subjects too large to fit into one shot.

Tilt: A camera move that pivots the camera vertically, up or down, from a stationary position and height. Follows movement, contrasts differences in size between two subjects, or gives viewer point-of-view sense of a subject's height.

Tracking: Lateral camera movement aligned with moving subject; subject background appears to move. Camera should maintain regulated distance from subject.

Zoom: To change the focal length of a zoom lens, from wide-angle to telephoto, and vice versa. The technique of "Zooming in" increases the focal length toward the telephoto setting. "Zooming out" means to decrease the focal length toward the wide-angle setting.

Point of View (POV): Shot perspective in which the camera assumes the position of an actor, allowing viewers to see what the actor sees as if through his or her eyes.

Framing: Act of composing a shot in the camcorder's viewfinder for desired content, angle, and field of view—overall composition.

Abbreviations used in storyboarding:
LS: Long Shot
MS: Medium Shot
CU: Close-up
POV: Point of View
FX: Special Effect

Appendix N

Video Editing Cards & Appliances

Matrox Graphics, Inc.—www.matrox.com

Pinnacle Systems, Inc.—www.pinnaclesys.com

Canopus Corporation—www.canopus.com

Avid Technology, Inc.—www.avid.com

MacroSystem—www.casablanca.tv

Applied Magic—www.applied-magic.com

NewTek—www.newtek.com

Appendix O

Recommended Video Footage Resources

Artbeats*—www.artbeats.com

Digital Juice—www.digitaljuice.com

Highway Video*—www.highwayvideo.com

Fresh Out of the Box—www.abingdonpress.com

iWorship—www.integritymusic.com

North American Mission Board—
www.namb.com/essentials/

Video Animation*—www.videoanimation.com

Video Scriptures*—www.video4worship.com

Worship Scapes*—www.royaltyfreestuff.com

* *Free samples are available on the DVD in the* **Bonus Resources** *folder.*

Appendix P
Recommended Reading

Media Ministry

Fields, Doug and James, Eddie, *Videos That Teach, Volumes 1 & 2* (Grand Rapids: Zondervan Publishing, 1999 and 2002).

Miller, Kim, *Handbook for Multisensory Worship, Volumes 1 & 2* (Nashville: Abingdon Press, 1999 and 2000).

Slaughter, Michael, *Out on the Edge* (Nashville: Abingdon Press, 1998).

Wilson, Len and Moore, Jason, *The Wired Church* (Nashville: Abingdon Press, 1999).

Wilson, Len and Moore, Jason, *Digital Storytellers* (Nashville: Abingdon Press, 2002).

Wilson, Len and Moore, Jason, *Fresh Out of the Box, Vol.1 & 2* (Nashville: Abingdon Press, 2002).

PowerPoint

Lowe, Doug, *PowerPoint 2002 for Dummies* (Hoboken: John Wiley & Sons, 2001).

Perspection, Inc., *Microsoft PowerPoint Version 2002 Step by Step* (Redmond: Microsoft Press, 2001).

Photoshop

Adobe Creative Team, *Adobe Photoshop 7.0 Classroom in a Book* (Adobe Press, 2002). (www.adobe.com)

Kelby, Scott, *Adobe Photoshop 7.0 Down & Dirty Tricks* (Indianapolis: New Riders Publishing, 2002). (www.newriders.com)

Matthews, Lisa, *Adobe Photoshop Elements 2.0 Idea Kit* (Adobe Press, 2002). (www.adobe.com)

Premiere

Adobe Creative Team, *Adobe Premiere 6.5 Classroom in a Book* (Adobe Press, 2002). (www.adobe.com)

Morris, Tee and Oakley, Steve, *Premiere 6.5 Power!* (Boston: Muska & Lipman). (www.muskalipman.com)

Appendix Q

Royalty-Free Music Resources

David Delgado—www.daviddelgado.com

Digital Juice—www.digitaljuice.com

SmartSound—www.smartsound.com

Music2Hues—www.music2hues.com

Media-Tracks—www.media-tracks.com

Network Music—www.networkmusic.com

Sound Dogs—www.sounddogs.com

Sound FX—www.soundfx.com

Using the DVD

Playing the DVD

Windows: To begin playing the DVD, simply insert the disk into your drive. The program should automatically launch and go to the **Main Menu**. The **Main Menu** provides the main tool for navigating and accessing content on the DVD. Click the gold buttons located on the left of the text to initiate an action (the text itself is not "hot").

If the disk does not begin playing for some reason, you can manually launch the program by locating it on the disk. In Windows, go to **Windows Explorer**, locate the disk icon, and select it to see the contents of the DVD. Find the **mmme.exe** file and double-click it to launch the program.

Macintosh: Double-click the disk icon and locate the **mmmeOS9** and **mmmeOSX** files. Double-click the version you need to launch the program.

For Technical Support, call **615-749-6777**, Mon.–Fri., 8:00 A.M.–5:00 P.M., CST.

System Requirements

The DVD was created using Macromedia® Director® The following are the recommended minimum playback requirements for using the DVD:

Windows
- Pentium II, 600 MHz or higher
- Windows 98, ME, NT4, 2000, XP
- 128MB of RAM; 256 recommended
- DVD-ROM drive
- Apple QuickTime® 5.x or higher

Macintosh
- Power Macintosh G3 or higher
- MAC OS 9.x to 10.x
- 128MB of RAM; 256 recommended
- DVD-ROM drive
- Apple QuickTime® 5.x or higher

Monitor Resolution

For best performance, your monitor resolution needs to be set at 1024 x 768. To change your monitor setting on your computer, refer to the help file or the documentation for your operating system.

Installing the Workshop Files

The workshop files contain files that you will use to complete the workshop exercises. Installing these files will provide you with the source material (graphics, PowerPoint files, sound files, and video clips) to create the projects demonstrated on the videos. You should install these *before* beginning work on the exercises. In **Windows**, a self-extracting zip file (.exe) will be launched when you click **Install Workshop Files**. Follow the onscreen instructions to complete the installation. These files will be saved on your hard drive in a folder called *Media Ministry Made Easy*.

On the **Macintosh**, a self-extracting Stuffit® file will be launched, and the **Save** dialog box will be opened. Choose the location where you want the folder to be saved (the default folder name will be *Media Ministry Made Easy* and the default location will be the desktop). Click **Save** to continue unstuffing and copying the files to your hard drive.

Playing Movies

The DVD contains three practical, hands-on videos that take the user step-by-step through the primary software tools used in media ministry. To play the movies, you will need to have the Apple QuickTime® player (version 5.x or higher), including the **Authoring Support** component, installed on your computer. If this component is not present on your computer, you will be alerted when you try to play a movie and be prompted to update the QuickTime player with this component. Click **OK** to enable QuickTime to install **Authoring Support** from the Apple website.

If you do not have QuickTime installed, it has been included on the DVD. Simply browse to the folder **QuickTime 5 Installers** by using Windows Explorer or by double-clicking the DVD icon on your desktop (Macintosh). Open the folder and select the folder inside that contains the installer for your computer platform. Double-click the **QuickTime Installer** to begin the installation. *Note: During the installation process, be sure to select the* ***Recommended*** *installation, which is the default. If you would prefer to use the* ***Custom*** *installation option, you will need to include the* ***Authoring Support*** *component in the installation in order to play the* ***MMME*** *movies.*

Installing Trial Software & Bonus Resources

Trial versions of Adobe Photoshop and Adobe Premiere have been included on the DVD. Trial versions of some of the leading worship software and presentation packages have also been included on the DVD. (*All worship software trials included are for Windows. Only Prologue SundayPlus has an available version for the Macintosh platform. You can obtain a trial version by contacting the company.*) These trials are fully functional, but are operational for a limited period. Make sure you do not install them until you are ready to work on the exercises or evaluate the software.

Note: If you encounter a problem installing any trial software included on the DVD, please check the company's website for information about available support for trial versions; Abingdon Press cannot provide support for software from other companies.

Windows: To install a trial, click the button beside the corresponding software program to launch the installation program. Follow the onscreen prompts to complete the installation.

Macintosh: Click the **Install Trial Software** button at the bottom of the screen to open the **Adobe Software Trials** folder. Select either the Photoshop or Premiere installer to begin installation of the trial. Follow the onscreen prompts to complete the installation.

The **Bonus Resources** folder contains sample video clips, audio files, and graphics you can customize for your own presentations. Like the workshop files, this folder will be installed using a self-extracting zip file (Win) or Stuffit file (Mac). See the paragraph on "Installing the Workshop Files" above for more information.